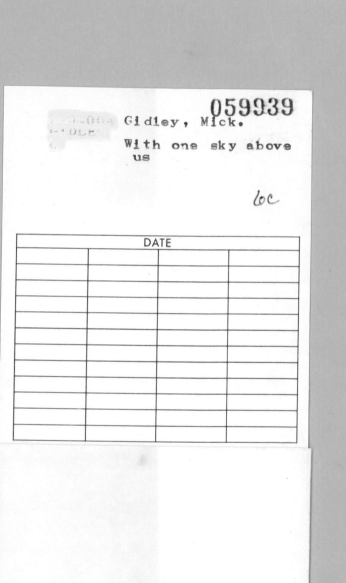

059939

Gidley, Mick.

With one sky above
us

6c

DATE			

CUP
RLIN

© THE BAKER &

NPLC99

With One Sky Above Us

With One Sky Above Us

Life on an Indian Reservation at the Turn of the Century

M Gidley

Photographs by Dr Edward H. Latham
U.S. Indian Agency Physician

G.P. Putnam's Sons
New York

For our children, Ruth and Ben.

1 Half-title page: tepees, Nespelem
2 Title page: horseman

A  book

Edited, designed and produced by
Webb & Bower (Publishers) Limited
Exeter, England

Designed by Vic Giolitto

Published in the USA 1979 by
G.P. Putnam's Sons
New York

Typesetting and monochrome origination by
Keyspools Limited, Golborne, Lancs

Printed and bound in Great Britain at
William Clowes & Sons Limited
Beccles and London

Contents

List of Plates

*Whenever the white man treats the Indians as they
treat each other, then we shall have no more wars.
We shall all be alike – brothers of one father and
mother, with one sky above and one country around
us, and one government for all. Then the Great
Spirit Chief who rules above will smile upon this
land, and send rain to wash out the bloody spots
made by brothers' hands upon the face of the earth.*

Chief Joseph, 1879

Preface and Acknowledgements

This book was made possible by the conjunction of a number of fortuitous circumstances. The award of an American Council of Learned Societies American Studies Fellowship for 1976–7 made it possible for me to conduct research at the University of Washington, Seattle. The University of Exeter, England, granted me financial help and study leave for the same period. The Thomas Burke Memorial Washington State Museum at the University of Washington kindly gave me a base to work. The Lindsley Collection of Dr E. H. Latham's negatives was acquired by the Photography Collection, Suzzallo Library, University of Washington, precisely while I was attempting to find out more about Dr Latham's photographs.

Then, once I had the bit between my teeth, a number of institutions kindly allowed me the use of their excellent facilities: the Federal Archives and Records Center, Seattle; the Eastern Washington State Historical Society Library, Spokane; the Reference Section, Spokane Public Library; the History Department, Seattle Public Library; the Manuscript, Archives and Special Collections Division, Washington State University, Pullman; the Library of the Rainier Club, Seattle; and, of course, the University Archives, the Manuscript Division and the Northwest Collection at the University of Washington.

In the summer of 1978 the award of Fellowships by the British Academy and the American Philosophical Society enabled me to return to the United States and to visit the National Archives and the National Anthropological Archives in Washington, D.C., and the Library of the Washington State Historical Society, Tacoma. Also, I received assistance by mail from the Montana Historical Society, Helena; the Ohio Historical Society, Columbus; Special Collections, University of Cincinnati Library, Cincinnati; and the Cincinnati Historical Society. I would like to thank all these institutions for allowing me to consult their collections. Where appropriate, materials reproduced in this book from these collections are cited in the section on Sources; at this point I would like to express my gratitude formally for permission to publish them.

Many individuals have given most generously to me of their time, hospitality, encouragement, or knowledge—or, often, a combination of these. I would like to mention all of them by name here, but must be content with the following: Terry Abraham, Dennis Anderson, Annie Cercle, Leonard Eshom, Maurice Evans, Adelin Fredin, Susan Harshberger, Robert Hitchman, Bill Holm, Janet Ibbetson, Andrew Johnson, Ellis Jones, Gary Lundell, Charles and Ann McLaughlin, Robert Monroe, James Murphy, James Nason, Annie Owhi, George Quimby, Robert Ruby, Lewis Saum, Sandra Skinner, Addie Thomas, Anne Van Camp, Elijah Williams.

None of these people should be considered responsible for any errors that I have made. That there are some I can be almost certain. I am acutely conscious that I am essentially a stranger among both Native and white Americans; I hope my mistakes of fact or judgement in this book will be forgiven with the same grace that my ignorance and questions in person have always been treated.

My family have been unfailingly supportive and good company, even when I have been bad-tempered or even—in spirit at least—absent. It is not any mere idle and conventional addition here to say that without the love and presence of Nancy, my wife, this book would not have been completed.

Mick Gidley
Exeter, December 1978

Introduction

On Christmas Day in 1904 the leading illustrated feature article in the prominent Portland newspaper, *The Oregon Sunday Journal*, concluded with these words: "Dr. Latham ... has without doubt the finest collection of Indian photographs in the Northwest." At a time when Edward S. Curtis of Seattle was beginning to enjoy a considerable reputation as a Northwest photographer of Indians, and when Major Lee Moorhouse of Pendleton, Oregon, was at the height of his fame in this domain, the judgement of the writer of this article, Vella Winner, represents high praise indeed. The article, though actually about "Choosing Chief Joseph's Successor", was liberally sprinkled with quotations from Dr Latham and surmounted by a group of his pictures—two portraits of Chief Joseph, a wedding picture of the prominent Nez Perce leader William Andrews, a shot of two Indian children, and a view of Chief Joseph's tepees. Though Latham seems to have sold odd prints and albums of his Indian pictures to friends and admirers from at least 1903, the article in *The Oregon Sunday Journal* probably marks the apex of his reputation as a photographer. Certainly, from then on—until today—his work sank into oblivion.

As an historical personage, however, Dr Edward H. Latham has achieved his portion of immortality. Chief Joseph, credited with the leadership of his

3 Dr Edward H. Latham, summer, 1901, by Frank F. Avery

4 Chief Joseph in war costume, 1903. In Latham's inimitable spelling, the note in his handwriting on this picture reads: "Copywrighted May 1903 By Dr. Edward H. Latham." There are at least two distinct images of Joseph taken on the same occasion which still survive; in the other there is no evidence of wind blowing his clothes. This is the picture that the Seattle *Post-Intelligencer* printed above Joseph's obituary and which caused such anger in Latham

people in the Nez Perce War of 1877 and eloquent spokesman thereafter from exile, has become a legendary figure, perhaps the most fabled of those Native American leaders that Alvin Josephy has termed "the patriot chiefs". Latham was the Indian Agency Physician at the time and place of Chief Joseph's death. When Joseph took leave of this life, on September 21, 1904, at Nespelem, Washington, on the Colville Reservation, it was Latham who was reported as stating that the Chief had died of "a broken heart". The statement was widely circulated at the time and soon achieved the status of an official diagnosis. It has been repeated again and again by historians. Some of the historians have attributed the judgement to a named source, either Latham himself or a later successor at Nespelem, a Dr Johnson, but most have credited it to "the doctor". At any rate, it has now acquired the force of myth. In fact, Latham was not actually present when Chief Joseph died, but he did believe that nostalgic longing for his ancestral home in Oregon's Wallowa Valley, his people's homeland before the 1877 war, was one of the ultimate causes of the Chief's heart failure. And he said so publicly in a newspaper item that appeared in the Spokane, Washington, daily *The Spokesman–Review* under the headline "Chief Joseph's End Due to His Grief".

In private Latham was rather more personally concerned over a related matter. In a state of some excitement, he wrote to Professor Edmond S. Meany, Head of the Department of History at the University of Washington in Seattle; in this letter, perhaps due to his agitation, his spelling and grammar (which will always be preserved here in quotations from his letters) proved even more calamitous than usual:

> I was not here at the time of Joseph's death and regret it very much indeed. He was buried before I returned, his people are all at Yakima gathering hops, upon their return they may have some doings but I do not think it will amount to much, if there is anything worth while I will try to get photoes. I think it very shabby in the PI to publish my copywrighted picture and not give me any credit of any kind.

The photograph of Joseph referred to in this letter (see plate 4) had been published by the Seattle *Post-Intelligencer* immediately above the Chief's obituary. It is the only one of Latham's pictures which has been quite widely reprinted but, in a further irony that would doubtless have infuriated the doctor, it has almost invariably been wrongly attributed to a photographer named T. W. Tolman (or, on occasion, Tollman). Even in the file of former copyright prints of Indian photographs at the National Anthropological Archives in Washington, D.C., it is attributed to Tolman, and a group of Dr Latham's photographs in the Montana Historical Society collection are also credited to this mysterious figure. Certain other Latham pictures have been copyrighted—and may even have appeared in print—under the name of another artist, a more recent photographer from the State of Washington, L. D. Lindsley; such likenesses include those in this book of Annie from Wenatchee (plate 48) and an intense young man (plate 82). It is likely that Lindsley befriended the older Latham after the latter's retirement to a small house on Washington's Lake Chelan, where Lindsley also had a residence, and thus acquired some of his negatives. In any case, most of the hundreds of images that Latham made were never published at all and very many must have perished altogether (see Chapter 4).

5 Nez Perce children, c1903.
This image was printed in
The Oregon Sunday Journal
under the title "Nez Perce
Papooses"

6 *Opposite* William Andrews
and bride, c1903. Andrews,
like many other figures in
these pictures, is wearing ear-
rings made of conch shells

7 Columbia women on horseback

This book has been made in the conviction that Latham's life and work can provide illumination. Latham deserves attention as a photographer, especially from an aesthetic point of view; this is the first account of his work and, of necessity, is exploratory and provisional. Latham is also historically noteworthy. Many books have been devoted to the Indian Wars, but very few to the reservation period, even though this extends into our own time. The story of the reservation era may be less glamorous than that of the Wars—indeed, it is one of deliberate cultural destruction—but it should be told. A small part of the story is told here by looking at just one reservation, the Colville Reservation—in national terms by no means famous—and essentially through the eyes of only one man, Dr Edward Latham.

The Colville Reservation is interesting in its own right, and, in some respects, might be considered a representative one. It was and is enormous. Situated in the arid uplands of eastern Washington and partly bounded by the Columbia River, it serves as home both to peoples indigenous to the area, such as the San Poils, and to tribes dumped there for riddance, such as Chief Moses' people, the Columbias. Several languages and cultures jostled there, and the various peoples responded differently to the rules of the U.S. federal government's Bureau of Indian Affairs as represented by the Agent and his staff. Latham probably knew the Nez Perce people best (and certainly more of his images of them survive), but he was acquainted with all the major groups.

8 Columbia River. The Colville Reservation is largely bounded by the Columbia. This view was probably made below Nespelem approaching the site of the present-day Chief Joseph Dam

Certain of the chiefs were distinguished or colorful figures, none more so than Chief Joseph, eloquent leader of the Nez Perces. At the turn of the century all Native Americans were placed at a critical point in their tribal lives: their traditional ways had been made untenable and they were expected to adjust to the white world.

Fortunately, Latham actually lived on the reservation and was interested enough to record with his camera the changing life all around him at Nespelem. In this he contrasts sharply with certain better known photographers of Indians, such as Edward S. Curtis and A. C. Vroman, who had to make special journeys to photograph their subjects, and even with a man like L. A. Huffman, who lived in a town near to the reservation he photographed in Montana. In fact, Latham is more strictly comparable with two of his own acquaintances: Lee Moorhouse of Pendleton near the Umatilla Reservation and Frank F. Avery, Superintendent of Schools on the Spokane Reservation, a man whose photographs have only recently been discovered, including two of Latham reproduced in this book. A fair number of Latham's firsthand views survive as negatives or prints. Also, since he was on the reservation in an official capacity for many years, a number of his letters could be found in the files of the Colville Reservation and Bureau of Indian Affairs in Seattle and Washington, D.C. As will become apparent, he proved to be a representative figure of his time and place, with representative views and biases. He was not actually as sympathetic to the Nez Perce people, for instance, as his oft-quoted verdict on Chief Joseph's death might lead us to conclude. Indeed, he often thought of the Chief as a cunning schemer and of his people as overlibidinous savages. This and others of his opinions have not been published and examined, and neither have his photographs. As presented here, virtually all for the first time, it is to be hoped that they offer insight into—and, in any case, literally a *view* of—certain aspects of reservation life at the turn of the century.

1 The Reservation

"I fancy that this is my Country"

In 1829, Speckled Snake, who was over a hundred years old, spoke as follows to his people: "I have listened to many talks from our great father. But they always began and ended in this—'Get a little further; you are too near me'." Speckled Snake was right. From the time of earliest white settlement in North America Native Americans had been losing their lands. Speckled Snake's own people, the Creeks, had once occupied a large portion of the southeastern states and the Creek Confederacy had been an influential political entity, sometimes acting as a broker between the British and other grasping European powers. As white settlement increased there was terrific pressure on the Creeks and on other southeastern tribes, such as the Cherokees, to remove themselves.

Whole tribes died out; some fled or simply dwindled away into the forests beyond the ends of advancing roads and settlements, while others, like the Pequots of New England, were erased by war. While "the great father" was Andrew Jackson it became official United States government policy to forcefully remove recalcitrant Indians from their lands and relocate them elsewhere—in "Indian Territory", the then unwanted tracts of land beyond the Mississippi River. In 1838 sixteen thousand Cherokees were removed westward by the army on what became known as the "Trail of Tears". A quarter died on the way.

In being pushed from their own traditional land base, each tribe was also forced to adopt new cultural patterns in order to survive as an entity. The Delawares, for example, in moving from the Atlantic seaboard to the edge of settlement became less farmers and more hunters and, since they had to fight with indigenous tribes for the new land they needed, more warlike. In states of greater and lesser organization, the Delawares moved from eastern Ohio to Indiana. In 1818 they ceded their lands there in exchange for territory in Missouri, but by 1829 this in turn was ceded for land in Kansas, from which base they traded far and wide. Meanwhile, other Delawares settled in Texas, accepting a reservation there in 1854. By 1866, however, along with the Kansas Delawares, the majority of them had to agree to one last removal, this time to former Cherokee land in Indian Territory.

The reservation system came into being to cope with the removal of Indians from the East, and during the latter half of the nineteenth century it came into force against western Indians. In the West the pace of change, however, was considerably accelerated; while it took Speckled Snake more than an average lifetime to see the beginning of the end, most western Indians experienced the whole transition from freedom and self-determination to restricted life on a government-controlled reservation in little more than a quarter-century. Indians, the Plains Indians especially, resisted white

9 Mounted warrior. This is a portrait of David Williams, a prominent Nez Perce. The spots painted on the horse are supposed to indicate the places where bullets struck the horse when it was shot from under its rider

10 A group of Snake River Indians. The title of this picture as used here is taken from an early identification by a white historian, Thomas Prosch. If it is accurate, the people depicted here are probably Bannocks, Shoshonean-speakers from eastern Oregon to the south. But an elderly present-day resident of the Colville Reservation called them a mixed group of Colvilles and Nez Perces from near Keller on the San Poil River. If this is so, the obvious sadness and distress in the faces may be due to the memorial events for relatives who had died during the preceding year which were held just prior to July 4 celebrations at Nespelem

11 Young woman with
beadwork, June 1905. This
woman is probably a
Nespelem

encroachment heroically, as is well known. But eventually, whatever the
course taken by a particular people, the end—as the following brief examples
show—was the same: the reservation.

The Northern Cheyennes ranged over a vast part of what is now southern
Montana, northern Wyoming and the Dakotas. They lived alongside the
Sioux with whom they had shared the great victory over General G. A.
Custer at the Battle of the Little Bighorn in 1876—and the subsequent defeat
at the hands of the avenging armies. It was decided that instead of being
granted a reservation of their own or with the Sioux they should be
transported to share a reservation with their distant cousins, the Southern
Cheyennes, in Indian Territory, now Oklahoma. They were marched
overland for three months and several died on the way. Down on the arid
southern plains, many more died of malaria and malnutrition. So, as Mari
Sandoz has told most compellingly in *Cheyenne Autumn*, the majority of the
survivors broke out of the reservation and headed northwards under Dull
Knife and Little Wolf. They were starving, pursued by several armies, and
winter descended as they journeyed. But they made it—only to be captured
and incarcerated at Fort Robinson, Nebraska; and, when they escaped, they
were hunted down like animals in the snow. Eventually, though, the tiny
remnant of the tribe was granted a reservation of its own in a fragment of its
own former territory in the southeastern corner of Montana.

The Navahos had a similar devastating experience when, after a protracted
campaign against them in the 1860s by Kit Carson, they were taken for several
years to an uninhabitable reservation. This was at Bosque Redondo in New
Mexico, far from their grazing lands in the Four Corners region of the
Southwest, far from their place of peach orchards and last retreat, Arizona's
Canyon de Chelly. Eventually they were allowed home, but to a reduced
territory that became their reservation. In comparison with other peoples,
however, the Navahos were singularly fortunate. The Comanches, who
formerly roamed the whole of the southern plains from Texas upwards,
received but a bitter portion of land in Oklahoma, as did their former allies to
the north, the Kiowas, and their former enemies, the Otos, the Caddos, and
the Osages. And Geronimo's Apaches had to scrape by on part of the
Oklahoma reservation originally set aside for the Comanches. Furthermore,
those peoples who fought alongside the U.S. Army fared no better: the Utes
who joined Carson against the Navahos were, in their turn, ousted from
Colorado and dumped in Utah; even the Crows, who scouted for Custer
against the Sioux and who harried the Nez Perces for General O. O. Howard,
received a reservation that was nowhere near the size of their natural domain.

In the Northwest, where Dr Latham was to practise his profession and take
his pictures, the story was the same. The Northwest, like California, was
extraordinarily rich in its representation of language families. To the far
northeast were the Algonquin-speaking Blackfeet, enemies to all of the
Plateau peoples featured in this book. Also to the northeast, and spilling over
into Canada, were the Kitunahan-speaking Kutenais with their beautiful bark
canoes. To the southeast were the Shoshonean Bannocks and Shoshonis,
enemies who were nevertheless traded with, sometimes as far north as The
Dalles on the Columbia River. In the south were the Lutuamian-speaking
Kalapooias of the Willamette Valley, the Klamaths of southern Oregon, and
the Modocs, whose courageous war against removal in the early 1870s caused
whites throughout the region to believe a general Indian uprising was

imminent. The great Athapascan-language family—which includes the Navahos in the Southwest and the Sarsis on the northern plains—was represented by tiny pockets of people, such as the Willapas, near the mouth of the Columbia, but they were rapidly being extinguished at the turn of the century.

On the coast to the far north were the Wakashan-speaking Kwakiutl and Nootka peoples, from whom many interior tribes had taken elements of the potlatch ceremony—the giving away of earthly goods, often after a death in the family. Also on the western seaboard, from Puget Sound down, were Salish-speaking tribes, such as the Clallams, Suquamishes and Snohomishes. Soon after the establishment of Washington Territory in 1853 its first governor, General Isaac Ingalls Stevens, made a series of treaties with these Coastal Salish peoples which almost totally extinguished their rights to their homelands; the new town of Seattle took both its name and title from one of the great chiefs of the region, Sealth or Seattle. War inevitably followed and these coastal tribes were crushed, coming out of it with but poor reservation plots which were eventually surrounded by a rapidly expanding white population and an economy in which they had no place. The lot of these peoples was borne in mind by the interior tribes when, very soon afterwards, they were called to councils with Stevens. Further south, from the mouth of the Columbia and along its shores to The Dalles, were bands of the Chinookan-language group. The Chinooks were great traders, as befitted their position on the Columbia, the principal artery of trade in the region. However, as the fur trade with whites was established, and then missions and settlers, the Chinooks were decimated from the 1820s onwards by smallpox and influenza, diseases which were to continue to strike down interior tribes right into the twentieth century. Many individual Chinooks became absorbed by other tribes, including those of the interior. Their language, with elements from Nootka, became the basis of the Chinook jargon. The jargon, with words taken from English and French, became the lingua franca of the whole Indian Pacific Northwest. Any whites dealing with Indians, such as Latham, had to learn it.

The two language groups with the largest number of speakers in the interior were the Salishan and Shahaptian families. Furthest east of the Salishan tribes were the Flatheads of western Montana. They were great allies of both other Salish speakers and Shahaptian speakers from the west when these fellow Plateau peoples ventured over the Rockies to hunt buffalo. It was their lot, despite the fact that many of them had become practising Christians and all had enjoyed friendly relations with whites, to be placed by Governor Stevens on a reservation which was a mere fraction of their former hunting grounds. At the same treaty council with Stevens, in 1855, their neighbors to the west, the Pend d'Oreilles, also accepted the inevitable reservation. The Coeur d'Alenes, on the other hand, resisted. At first they were successful: in 1858 they defeated a detachment of regular troops under Lieutenant Colonel Edward J. Steptoe. But before long another army, with much sophisticated weaponry and the ruthless Colonel George H. Wright in command, was sent to avenge the defeat. It did so, with much hanging of innocent Indians. The Coeur d'Alenes submitted to reservation life.

The Colville Reservation was established in 1872. It was bounded by the Canadian border to the north, the Okanogan River to the west and the Columbia to the south and east. Thus, although not all of them signed treaties

formally accepting the reservation, a number of Salishan tribes found they had
an invisible wall around them; these included the Nespelems, the San Poils,
the Lakes and, partially at least, the Okanogans and the Colvilles. Each of
these peoples responded somewhat differently to a similar plight. The
Nespelems, who were more or less permanently settled in the Nespelem
Valley, were a small, fairly isolated group renowned for their fine beadwork.
Under their chief Quequetas, and, to a certain extent, under the influence of
Chief Skolaskin of the San Poils, they kept themselves to themselves, resisted
incursions on to their lands—including, as will be seen, those of other
Indians—and tried to live in their traditional ways.

Skolaskin of the San Poils kept his people to a rigorous course: they would
neither fight the white man nor make treaties with him, and they would not
adopt his ways. In time this put him politically on the opposite side from all
the other chiefs on the reservation, so that the Bureau of Indian Affairs saw
him as a troublemaker. In 1889 he was arrested and jailed, without trial, at
Alcatraz in San Francisco Bay. In his absence the North Half of the Colville
Reservation was sold and opened up for settlement, so that when he returned
to it in 1892 he was incensed at what he viewed as a betrayal. Despite the fact
that he had pledged to keep the peace, he urged the Okanogans and others to

12 Woman with saddle
horse. This Colville woman is
holding a tiny puppy

31

13 Columbia Joe and family, July 4, 1901. Columbia Joe, who was probably an Okanogan, is wearing an angora-goat "medicine hat". The tapaderos (long stirrups) and high saddle were both popular at the turn of the century

resist the opening. Their efforts were to no avail, and furthermore the Indians received no payment for the sale of their land.

The Lake people to the north were more pliant, especially under Chief Barnaby, who appears to have been attracted by white notions of wealth. After the North Half was sold many of his people drifted southward, eventually taking up allotments on the South Half of the reservation. Like the Colvilles, they had long had contact with whites and many were practising Christians.

The Okanogans were also largely Christian. Their principal chief, Tonasket, habitually thought that the only way to secure the future of his tribe was to accede always to the white man's desires—and, on occasion, he even turned against other Indians to this end. Together with fellow Okanogan Chief Sarsopkin, who was much less pro-white, and Chief Moses of the Columbias, he visited Washington, D.C., and was successful in being granted a mill and a school for his people and a small annuity for himself. When Tonasket died in 1891, Sarsopkin himself having already died after a drunken spree, Antwine, a much younger chief, was left as the major influence among the Okanogans. In his earliest years, Sarsopkin had opposed white incursions into the Northwest with force, but, like Tonasket, as he became a successful cattle raiser, he came to feel that he and the Okanogans could survive only in the larger economy of the white man. Antwine continued in this line. At the sale

of the North Half, he was the first to sign, which perhaps indicates the degree to which he had faith in the good intentions of the government. Thus the Okanogans, too, if they were to have any refuge from white settlers, had to seek it thereafter on the increasingly crowded South Half.

There were two other significant Salish-speaking tribes which were not indigenous to the land which became the Colville Reservation, even though they had often hunted there. These were the Spokanes and the Columbias. The Spokanes, under Chiefs Spokane Garry and Lot, were fortunate enough to receive some of their own territory just to the southeast of the Colville Reservation as their own reservation. However, like the Coeur d'Alene Reservation and the tiny Kalispel Reservation, both in Idaho, it was administered by the same Agent as the Colville Reservation and for many years shared the same employees, including Dr Latham.

The Columbias, under Chief Moses, were less fortunate. They had been more nomadic than some of the other Salish speakers, moving over the whole of the middle Columbia region, and were loath to submit to restriction to any small part of it. Ultimately, Moses accepted a reservation for his people to the west of the Colville Reservation, but it was already being settled by white cattlemen and he never lived on it. Before long it was sold and his people accepted allocations on the Colville Reservation in the Nespelem Valley. Some of the Columbia sub-bands never willingly accepted, including the

15 Young woman with
cornhusk bag. This woman is
probably a Wenatchee and
the first wife of a man named
Willie Nampoya

Wenatchees and the Chelans under Innomoseecha Bill and Long Jim. In time,
however, the remnants of these small bands were run off their lands by local
settlers and either became totally dispossessed or sought a place on the Colville
Reservation.

The other major language family of the Northwest was the Shahaptian.
This was represented by the Yakimas, the Klickitats, the Palouses, the
Umatillas, the Cayuses, the Walla Wallas, the Wanapums and the Nez Perces.
The Yakimas lived furthest west and, when Stevens made his unjust treaties
with the coastal tribes, they were the first to hear of it. Their principal leader in
opposing the presaged white domination was Kamiakin, who was partly
Palouse. In the councils of 1855 the Yakimas, like the other peoples, at first
agreed to reservations, and theirs was certainly a large one, including most of
their actual homelands. When white settlement started on their land before
the treaty had even been ratified, however, Kamiakin led them to war. They
killed an Indian Agent and, in the skirmishes that followed, fought alongside
other tribes. At first they were victorious, but in the end were divided and
defeated. Those who had most strongly resisted were scattered and made
destitute. These included the great Kamiakin who, wounded in the battle with
Colonel Wright, escaped to Canada. Later he ventured back to the United
States and lived with the Crows before returning to his father's people, the
Palouses. He died in 1878. Some of his children and followers, including one
son, Tomeo, eventually chose to live on the Colville Reservation rather than
take an allocation on the Yakima Reservation. One of his direct descendants,
Cleveland Kamiakin, survived well into the twentieth century and certainly
outlived his doctor, Edward Latham.

The Umatillas were more prepared to accept a reservation according to the
terms of the 1855 treaty with Stevens, partly because it was to be situated on
their home territory, the Umatilla Valley in Oregon. Nevertheless, they were
to share it with the Cayuses and the Walla Wallas. The Palouses to the north of
them, like the Klickitats, were to lose their own grazing lands entirely and
were supposed to move on to the Yakima Reservation, just as the Cayuses and
Walla Wallas were to join the Umatillas. All these tribes, therefore, fought
vigorously in the campaigns which followed the treaty. When the wars were
over certain individual Umatillas were so unhappy that during the 1870s they
sought new homes on the Colville Reservation and settled permanently
between Moses' people on the Nespelem and, to Skolaskin's annoyance, the
San Poils in the San Poil Valley.

The Cayuses, who were such renowned horsemen that their tribal name
came to be affixed to the horse itself, were not strictly members of the
Shahaptian language family but of a collateral descendant of it, so to speak, the
Waiilaputian. It was among them that the first mission in the Northwest was
built by Marcus Whitman in the 1830s. It was on them that the first severe
assertions of white dominance fell. It is not surprising that this led to the
disastrous Cayuse War when, in 1847, a group of them murdered Whitman
and others at the mission. At that time other tribes were reluctant to fight
against the whites, and the Cayuses took the full force of the white man's
vengeance: some of their men gave themselves up and were hanged, and
henceforth they found themselves bereft of their homeland. Eventually they
were allocated a place on the Umatilla Reservation; a few frequently visited
with their friends the Nez Perces at Nespelem and some may have settled
there. The Walla Wallas were closely associated with the Cayuses and also

experienced white aggression early; perhaps most significant of all, their great chief, Peo-peo Mox-mox, was murdered while a hostage in 1856. In time they virtually lost their tribal identity and merged with the Cayuses.

The Wanapums were closely associated with the Yakimas and were a relatively small tribe. However, one of them was to have a great influence on the way of life of—and the course of events for—many Northwest Indians. His name was Smohalla, and he was a prophet. There had been some tradition of messianic cults among most Northwest Indian peoples, but Smohalla was exceptionally effective in transmitting his particular version; it spread like a profound religious revival, which it was. Smohalla dreamed and he encouraged others to do so; in his dreams he foresaw the destruction of the world. In 1935, the anthropologist Leslie Spier wrote as follows in *The Prophet Dance of the Northwest*:

> It was held that a terrible convulsion of nature would destroy the world, when the Creator would restore the halcyon days of long ago and bring the dead to earth. A strict adherence to Indian dress and modes of life, and an upright life was enjoined on all true believers, for only such would participate in the final resurrection ... emphasis was laid on active animus toward the whites and their ways ... the whole point of the event was the destruction of the whites. Even the Earth-woman doctrine was taken so literally that no interference with her was permitted: there should be no parcelling of the land and above all no tilling of the soil.

Smohalla himself spoke as follows:

> My young men shall never work. Men who work cannot dream; and wisdom comes to us in dreams.
> You ask me to plough the ground! Shall I take a knife and tear my mother's breast? Then when I die she will not take me to her bosom to rest.
> You ask me to dig for stone! Shall I dig under her skin for her bones? Then when I die I cannot enter her body to be born again.
> You ask me to cut grass and make hay and sell it and be rich like white men! But how dare I cut off my mother's hair?

The ceremonies which Smohalla's "dreamers" participated in varied from tribe to tribe and changed slightly over the years, but they nearly always involved drumming and testimony, and often they were integrated into the remnants of the particular tribe's traditional ceremonial year; that is, the cult was at one and the same time a new thing brought about by the crisis of rapid white incursions into every sphere of life and a *reaffirmation* of traditional cultural patterns and values. At the turn of the century on the Colville Reservation there were many dreamers, especially in the Nespelem Valley where Latham was stationed.

Some of them were exiled Nez Perces, an extremely powerful Plateau people who resided in various bands over territory situated astraddle what are now the borders between Oregon, Washington, and Idaho. It was land through which Meriwether Lewis and William Clark explored in 1805, through which fur traders often passed and in which some of the earliest missions were established, including that of Henry Spalding in 1836. It was also land strategically placed and rich in natural resources, so the government wished to open it for development. Those Nez Perces who had become Christianized, mostly resident in Idaho and loyal to Chief Lawyer, were

17 Boy on a pony, with his father and mother. One elderly resident of Nespelem has identified these people as A-kis-kis (boy), Joe A-kis-kis, and his wife, a Palouse woman, Hal-a-mis

18 Three men. One contemporary historian, Thomas Prosch, titled his copy of this picture "Three Nez Perce Bucks", but a present-day resident of the Colville Reservation has identified them as, left to right, Walla-qua-mit, Nez Perce, Chu-ya, Umatilla, and Jim White, a much younger brother of White Bird, the legendary Nez Perce leader

19 *Opposite* Blacksmith and Indian assistant, Nespelem. C. M. Hinman was the blacksmith at Nespelem for a number of years from 1895. The brandmarks were those of the various horse-owning Indians on that part of the reservation. They sometimes branded horses on the neck under the mane. Chief Joseph's brand was the third from the left on the top row, below the T

prepared to accept a reservation centered on Lapwai, Idaho. Other bands, mostly non-Christian dreamers who were led by White Bird, Toohoolhoolzote and Joseph, refused to sign treaties giving up their lands. After much coercion by General Oliver Otis Howard and others, they did eventually agree to move on to the Nez Perce Reservation in Idaho. Inevitably there was terrible bitterness and rage; it erupted into violence, and the Nez Perce War began. Joseph's people, from the Wallowa Valley in northeastern Oregon, were the most reluctant of warriors. The non-treaty bands were all joined by Chief Looking Glass, who had initially also been in favor of peace. The brilliance and bravery of their campaign is legendary. But in the end the Nez Perce side consisted not just of warriors but of whole families, including the elderly and children; they were harried by three armies and they were a thousand miles from home with winter coming on. Looking Glass, Toohoolhoolzote, Joseph's brother Ollokot—and many others—were all killed, so Joseph surrendered.

Those Nez Perces who did not escape to Canada, like White Bird, were transported to Indian Territory. Many died there in what they came to call "the hot place", but they were not allowed to return to the Northwest until nearly ten years later, in 1885. About half the survivors were sent to Lapwai, but almost all the dreamers and virtually all of Joseph's Wallowa band were parcelled off to the Colville Reservation in eastern Washington.

Some of the Salish tribes did not want the Nez Perces there at all, and when, at the encouragement of Chief Moses, they were settled in the Nespelem

Valley, the Nespelems and the San Poils were furious. Skolaskin led a band of warriors to oppose the settlement, and the Agent, Major R. K. Gwydir, had to call in troops. This was but an omen of the continued ill-fortune that the Nez Perces were to experience at Nespelem. The most tragic outcome was the inexorable, if gradual, erosion of their traditional culture. Joseph always hoped to return to the Wallowa, but many of his people inevitably came to accept the Nespelem Valley as home. The dreamers would not farm, yet a life of hunting, free roaming and ranging was impossible. They were largely dependent on government issues for food; many lost their self-respect, they were in a poor state of health, and alcohol was readily available to corrupt those who, unlike Joseph himself, found themselves using it to transport them mentally from their plight.

In a sense, with the dumping of the Nez Perces at Nespelem, the Colville Reservation was complete. Concurrently, except for sporadic troubles both in the Northwest and elsewhere—one of which led to the massacre of Sioux at Wounded Knee in 1890—Indian resistance was over. Speckled Snake's vision, spoken in 1829, was verified:

> ... when the white man had warmed himself before the Indians' fire and filled himself with their hominy, he became very large. With a step he bestrode the mountains, and his feet covered the plains and the valleys. His hand grasped the eastern and the western sea, and his head rested on the moon. Then he became our Great Father. He loved his red children, and he said, "Get a little further, lest I tread on thee ..."

During the period from 1875 to 1925, the "great father" was not content simply to leave his red children alone in their allocated spaces. Every effort was made by the Bureau of Indian Affairs and its employees to force Native Americans into becoming first wards of the government, then part of the mainstream of American life. Since they could no longer sustain life fully by traditional means, such as hunting, they were made wards by being dependent on the government for farming supplies, sawmills, blacksmith's shops, and the like. That is why certain peoples, such as the San Poils and the Nespelems, who could survive by fishing and vegetable growing, insisted on paying for whatever provisions they took: this guaranteed them a fragile degree of autonomy. Some people were dependent on the government for much of the very food they put in their mouths; the Nez Perces, for instance, even had they been able to farm, were settled the first year at Nespelem too late to do any planting which would have done them any good. And sometimes the beef rations or the seedlings for sowing either did not arrive or were not distributed. Malnutrition—even starvation—were not uncommon on the reservation, especially among the Nez Perces.

On occasion food was deliberately withheld in order to coerce a people into a particular course of action. Thus, in 1901 Joseph and his people were refused their beef rations because the Chief opposed the sending of Nez Perce children away to boarding school at Fort Spokane. Education, of course, was to be the primary instrument in the making over of "Indians"—as the word was pejoratively used—into appropriate members of the wider American community. While Native Americans were not to be granted formal citizenship of the United States until 1924, they were encouraged at the turn of the century to wear "citizens'" dress, to cut off their braids, and to live in fixed houses. To this end government day schools were established at various

42

21 Fort Spokane. Built from about 1880, this army fort was abandoned in 1898, and later converted into a boarding school for Indian children

points on the reservation, including Tonasket and Nespelem. The first one at Nespelem burned down, but it was eventually rebuilt and though it was the subject of a rapid turnover of teachers, numerous closures and openings, the opposition of Joseph, or Moses, or both, it survived to teach the white man's ways to the children of the Nespelem Valley.

For a period after 1901 the day school was considered insufficient; children were sent to the boarding school made out of the converted army buildings of Fort Spokane. The buildings may have ceased to belong to the army, but military discipline prevailed at the school. Children worked on the grounds in detachments, they were lined up on the old parade square for roll call and exercises, the speaking of native languages and the Chinook jargon was punished by beating, and the wearing of shoes was compulsory. It is doubtless true that to survive in twentieth-century America, the acquisition of English was important, but the overwhelming emphasis was negative. The job of the school was to crush the Indian inside each child: "... the first step to be taken toward civilization, toward teaching the Indians the mischief and folly of continuing in their barbarous practices", wrote Commissioner of Indian Affairs J. D. C. Atkins in 1885, "is to teach them the English language". So it happened that a generation of children was urged to feel shame and revulsion towards its parents.

In traditional Plateau cultures women rather than men wielded axes in cutting down pines for lodge poles or dead branches for firewood, but under the new dispensation it was men who were rewarded if they logged the forests

22 *Opposite above* Tepee made of rushes. This was a traditional form of shelter for many Plateau peoples

23 *Opposite below* The saw and grist mill at Nespelem, c1901

24 Raising a flag pole with an ox team, Nespelem (1). The flagpole and weathervane is being raised by pulley; if the title of the picture is accurate, the ox team will shortly take the strain now being taken up by the line of men

to build houses; they were encouraged to bring the logs down to the new mill to be sawn into planks. The Nez Perces and the Columbias were used to a semi-nomadic life and did not take kindly to the new order. The government went so far as to build a house for Joseph, but he preferred to abide by his tepees.

In the cause of development and civilization, groups of Indians were hired as day or permanent laborers—levelling wagon roads, building houses and bridges, and, perhaps most significant of all, constructing ferries across the numerous major rivers. Some of this construction work was undertaken under contract by private companies and some was initiated by the Agent and his staff. The ferry at Moses' Crossing was built in the early 1890s by Henry M. Steele, a U.S. Indian Service farmer. The Columbia was undammed then, wild and liable to flood; it did so while the ferry was under construction and swept much of the timber down the wide reaches of the river. It was precisely because of this turbulence that the ferries were so vital, and they undoubtedly did lessen the number of Indians drowned at the various crossing points. Also, they enabled wagons to be brought on to the reservation, and larger machines, such as a thresher for the mill, and boxes of drugs for the doctor. But, above all, they reduced the isolation of the Indians from expanding centers of white civilization in the region and brought more whites to the reservation; the latter, as will be seen, would ultimately help to make the reservation less secure for Indians.

If the schoolteacher was intended to Americanize the younger generation, the farmer was in day-to-day contact with the adult generation: as well as issuing equipment and rations, it was his job to teach farming methods, to inculcate the proposed means of support. Obviously, such a man had to be aware of the aboriginal means of support he was attempting to supplant, but

25 *Opposite* Raising a flag pole with an ox team, Nespelem (2)

46

26 Nez Perce medicine
dance, with Two Moons.
Two Moons, seen here
dancing on the right, was the
principal shaman or medicine
man of the Nez Perces at
Nespelem. The Nez Perces
had much faith in their
medicine man and at first
they totally resisted treatment
by white doctors

27 Keller Ferry. This ferry, especially designed for crossing rapid water, was at the mouth of the San Poil River, where it joins the Columbia. Like the ferry at Barry or Moses' Crossing, this was an important entrance to the reservation across the Columbia

28 *Opposite* Indian man in angora chaps, two young women, and tepee. Angora chaps were very popular at the turn of the century. It is likely that the young man served as a cowboy for one of the white farmers who leased grazing land on the reservation

he would tend to give his guidance to those who would use it and did not, therefore, need to be in conflict. The doctor, on the other hand, had to confront native practices head-on, and at their most sensitive point.

The Bureau of Indian Affairs recognized this and vociferously encouraged its physicians to wean patients away from the "medicine man", to perpetually undermine that person's role and, ultimately, to supplant him. All the tribes on the reservation who had resisted becoming Christians—albeit in different ways—were nevertheless intensely religious, all believing that it was fundamental for a human being to observe the larger laws of the universe, to be in a right relationship with the earth, to have respect for the sanctity of all life. There were many shamans or medicine men: the Nez Perces had Two Moons, Moses' Columbias had Quiotsa, Tompasque (or Timpasket, as Latham spelt it) and Snawtonic, and Skolaskin himself often ministered to the San Poils. The practice which most enraged white doctors was the sweat bath, and their annoyance is easily understandable when smallpox victims were urged to sweat and then dip themselves in the freezing waters of the Nespelem. But the sweat lodge was a prominent feature of Plateau and Plains culture; the sweat was intended to purify body and mind. So the attempt to eradicate the sweat lodge was another effort to destroy the Indianness of Indian life.

In fact, towards the end of the nineteenth century courts for the trial of "Indian offenses" were established and various aspects of Native American culture were designated "crimes". In the regulations drawn up in 1892 by

50

30 *Opposite* Three young women with a bear. Plateau peoples frequently had young bears as pets; they also kept young coyotes, foxes, wolves, and deer, as well as dogs, crows, magpies and geese. Some families also reared eagles for their tail feathers

Commissioner of Indian Affairs, Thomas J. Morgan, these crimes included various dances, plural marriages, intoxication, refusal to engage on road-building duty or other "habits of industry" and, of course, the "practices of medicine men". This offense was described as follows:

> Any Indian who shall engage in the practices of so-called medicine men, or who shall resort to any artifice or device to keep the Indians of the reservation from adopting and following civilized habits and pursuits, or shall adopt any means to prevent the attendance of children at school, or shall use any arts of a conjurer to prevent Indians from abandoning their barbarous rites and customs, shall be deemed to be guilty of an offense, and upon conviction thereof, for the first offense shall be imprisoned for not less than ten and not more than thirty days.

Clearly, the much-vaunted American constitutional right to freedom of worship did not extend to include Indians; but then, they were not considered citizens. And all this is doubly ironic in the light of the fact that genuine offenses against persons on the reservation were frequently not brought to any sort of trial. Before the arrival of the white man tribes had dealt with murderers within the tribe by banishment, and outside the tribe by

29 Burros and packer, Nespelem. This man, here fording the Nespelem at springtime, may have been a prospector

31 Two women, baby and
tepee. This tepee is of a
typical Plateau style

vengeance. On the reservation neither was possible. Indeed, such matters had
to be dealt with by the Agent or by a white court, and all too frequently white
courts would not trouble to go to the expense of trying an Indian accused of
nothing more serious than the killing of another Indian.

Offenses against property, on the other hand, whether white or Indian,
were severely dealt with whenever possible. This was because respect for
property and the acquisition of it by individual Indians was considered a most
effective manner of Americanization. Such thinking received classic
expression in action in the Allotment Act of 1887. This Act was intended to
break forever collective tribal stewardship or ownership of land. Indians were
to be allotted individual, family-sized farms, and the "surplus" reservation
land was to be opened to white settlement, the Indians receiving a token
payment for the surplus land. Obviously, this policy received much support
from real-estate interests and it led to the sale of over *half* the land owned by
Indians before it became law. Since so many of the allotments were
uneconomic as farming units in any case, and since the new individual owners
were unskilled in farming, many were leased to neighboring whites for
grazing purposes or sold outright. Forced to look after only the immediate
family unit—and unable to do even that—Indians on many reservations
became chronically poor and some were made homeless. The latter tended to
congregate around the Agencies and on the edges of towns, and too many
took the turning to skid row. More than ever they were dependent on the
government and on such seasonal labor that became available in the
expanding white economy outside. For those on the Colville Reservation this
meant hop picking in the Yakima Valley and fruit harvesting in the new
orchards that irrigation by damming of rivers was making possible.

On the Colville Reservation it was not only the Allotment Act which
attracted white speculators. There was also the lure of gold. For a time it
threatened to destroy the reservation altogether. After the North Half of the
reservation was sold off, the Bureau of Indian Affairs proved totally ineffective
in preventing incursions by prospectors on to the South Half. A store selling
provisions to the miners was set up at Nespelem and, when the historian of the
Northwest, Edmond S. Meany, visited the sub-Agency there in 1901 he
recorded that the herds of Indian ponies on the hillsides were constantly
startled by explosions caused by the invading gold-seekers. Some Indians,
including Joseph and Moses, feared that such activity would lead inexorably
to the sale of the South Half too.

This did not actually prove to be the case, but the Chiefs' anxiety was well-
founded. In general, the Bureau was notoriously corrupt, and the
administration of the Colville Reservation was such that the confidence of the
Indians in it could not be expected to be very great. There were numerous
instances of government employees known to be trafficking in whisky. It was
common knowledge to settlers round about that certain officials would turn a
blind eye not only to illegal prospecting, but to illegal, unpaid-for grazing.
And individual Agents were not blameless. Until its removal to Nespelem in
the second decade of the twentieth century, the Agency itself was located at
points just on or off the reservation—Chewelah, Miles, Fort Spokane,
Spokane—and there was no way for the best of Agents to be fully informed of
all that was happening in so vast an area. But some made little effort to find
out, and certainly never visited the distant Nespelem Valley. Others were too
busy running their own businesses and conducted Agency affairs only as a

sideline. And some were positively corrupt; to give but two examples, both John W. Bubb, in 1896, and Albert M. Anderson, in 1904, were removed from their posts after discoveries of financial irregularities. Anderson had even gone so far, it was alleged, as to claim guardianships over Indian children and then take the monies from leasing their allotments.

Of course, at the end of the line, Native American men and women had to adjust to their new way of life. Sometimes their leaders were reduced to indulging in tribalistic factions and endless political bickering. All too often their own adjustment was that described so vividly by William Brandon in *The American Heritage Book of Indians*:

> ... thousands of dispirited people killed time in the institutionalized slums of their reservations, becoming adept in the skills of wise old boys who have lived a long time in the orphanage. They learned how to wheedle and hoodwink the agency staff for the nickels and dimes in scraps of supplies that trickled down through the budget to their level, and how to give some point to a pointless existence by finding delight in unutterable trivia. And the friendly agents said in a fond way, "They're children". Unfriendly agents said, "Indolent, insolent, and uncivilizable" ...

But a surprising number found the strength to endure, to raise their children with a measure of pride, and even to prevail. Many of these were people who sustained a link with the tribal past, the traditional culture. Sometimes the link was sustained only in terms of material culture—a continuing delight

32 *Opposite* Young woman with cornhusk bag, June 1905

33 Parade, Women's Division, July 4, Nespelem, 1900s. Unfortunately, the negative from which this picture was taken is scratched. The hats with their zigzag designs worn by some of the women were very popular, especially among the Nez Perces

34 Start of the parade, Women's Division, July 4, Nespelem, 1900s

in the showing off of well-executed beading, the making of cornhusk baskets, a cradleboard prepared in the old manner, or the construction of a complex fishing weir at the right point on a fast-flowing stream. Many such items were totally of Plateau origin: the woven tule mats out of which lodges were often made, say, or the conical grass hats with zig-zag designs favored by many women. Others were partly a result of having acquired horses and a taste for aspects of Plains culture, such as catlinite pipes, eagle headdresses or flat parfleches for the transport of dried meat. But, whatever their origin, in the end they were more than merely bits and pieces of material culture: they inevitably carried a symbolic meaning. Thus, in some of the great potlatches held after deaths of prominent people, items of material culture which were no longer made were highly prized by both givers and receivers. The Columbias, for instance, had once made many fine stone implements, carved mortars and pestles, stone axes and adzes, so when Chief Moses died, examples of this work were distributed and treasured even though the white man's trade versions of such implements were the ones which were actually used.

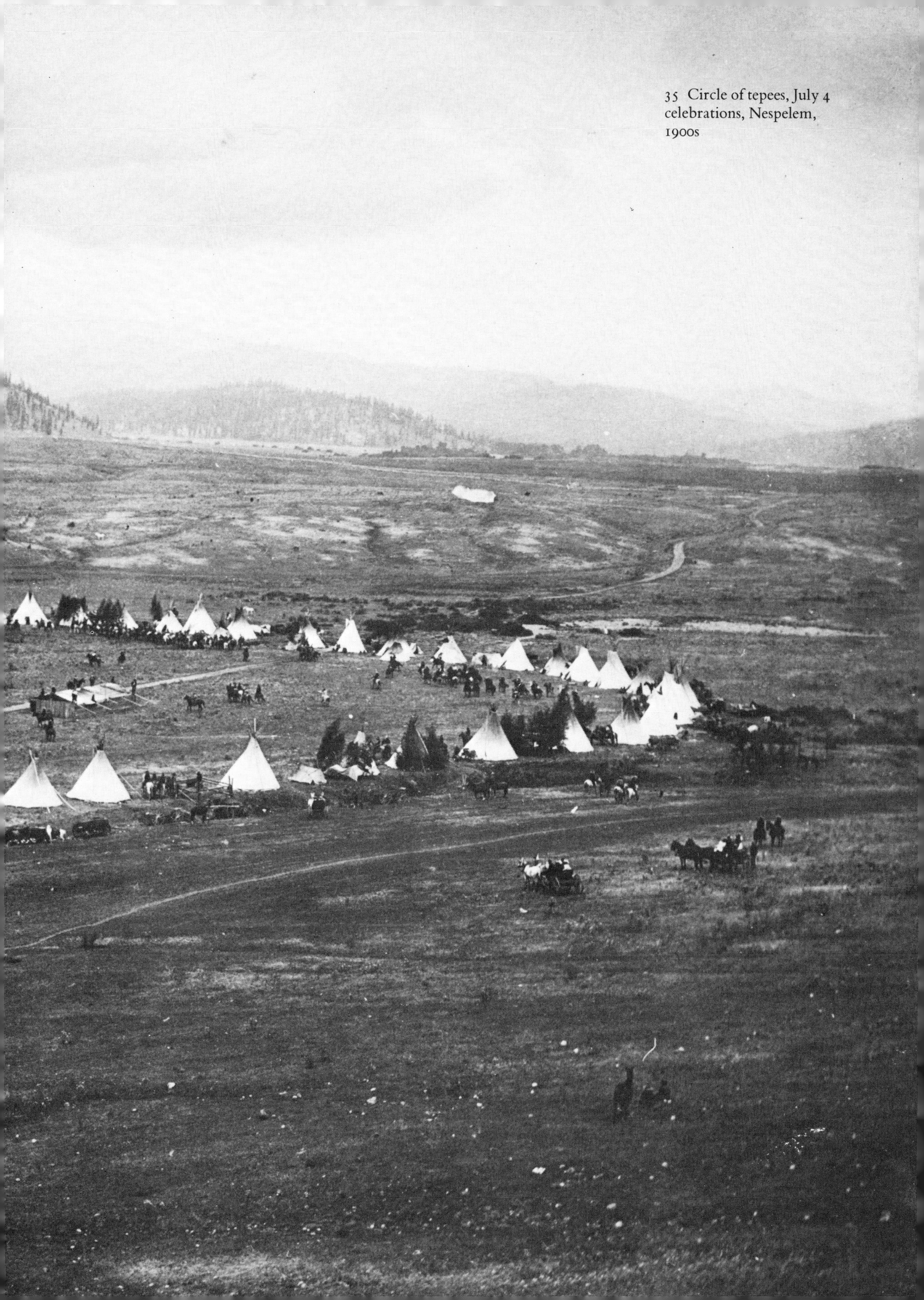

35 Circle of tepees, July 4 celebrations, Nespelem, 1900s

This indicates the sustaining importance not just of relatively rare ceremonial events, like potlatches, but, say, the annual July 4 celebrations held at Nespelem, especially by the Nez Perces. Brothers and cousins would come from the reservation in Idaho, and from further afield. All the items of the old material culture were worn and displayed. Gambling, which had been such a crucial factor in the lives of most Plateau men, was liberally indulged in. Horses were raced. Old games were played at a furious pace, always accompanied by much betting by both participants and spectators. And, of course, there were dances. And so it happened that an occasion ostensibly meant to celebrate the birthday of the United States became for the Nez Perces an affirmation of the tribe's cultural identity. Most of the tribes on the Colville Reservation had something similar, whether ceremonies to give thanks for the salmon or prophet services after the manner of Smohalla. And such festivities were an outward sign to all concerned that the "Indian" in these people was not yet dead.

2 The People

"They are not industrious"

There were some two thousand Indians living on the Colville Reservation during Dr Latham's time. In some ways this is not a large number; Chief Moses, on one of his visits to Washington, D.C., told a reporter that he fancied all his people could fit into the President's "back yard". Had the Colville terrain been less divisively mountainous and the winters less gripping, it is conceivable that Latham could have known virtually everyone by sight. But the winters were fierce and seemed to persist interminably, so even though Latham enjoyed horse trekking across the wilder parts, he appears to have kept his camera mainly for the summer and the Nespelem Valley. Therefore, there were many prominent non-Nespelem residents whose likenesses Latham missed. Unless it simply happened that his portraits of them have not survived—or, possibly, have not been identified as such—Chiefs Skolaskin, Komotelakia and Posahli of the San Poils, Tonasket and Antwine of the Okanogans, Lot of the Spokanes, Long Jim of the Chelans, and Barnaby of the Lake people were some of those that Latham never photographed. And in the Nespelem itself, where some six hundred people resided, he did not catch the likenesses of people he definitely knew very well, such as Snawtonic, one of Moses' shamans, or Blind Louis, Moses' brother, or Chief Quequetas of the Nespelems. But there were many others who did sit for him.

These were some of the chiefs:

Half-Sun, known to the whites as Moses, displaced warrior king
Cool-Cool-a-Weela, a man of many horses
Thunder Rolling in the Mountains, known to the whites as Joseph. Leader, spiritual force, eloquent speaker
Yellow Bull, Nez Perce war leader, blind and aged, yet still a skilful orator
David Williams, one-eyed chief who sought cooperation between the tribes

And these were some of the people:

Annie from Wenatchee
Charlie Wilpocken, laborer and traditionalist
Alice, daughter of Yellow Wolf
Chica-ma-poo, the oldest surviving Nez Perce at Nespelem and reported to have fought like a man during the Nez Perce War of 1877
Peo-peo Tholekt, politician
Lizzie Cayuse, "belle" of the Nez Perce

Their stories, all too barely and briefly told, follow.

Moses was a man of many names: Loolowskin, Quetalican or One Blue Horn, Sispilh Kalch or Seven Shirts, Sulkalthscosum. He was born in 1829 near the mouth of the Wenatchee River, possibly in that prehistoric river-bed valley now known as Moses' Coulee. He was a younger son of Sulkalthscosum or Half-Sun, head chief of the Sinkiuses or Columbias. The Half-Sun was not only a powerful man in his own tribe, which had once been much larger, but had great influence among all the Salish-speaking peoples between the Cascade Mountains to the west and the Rockies to the east. Moses would not have succeeded his father in the ordinary course of things, but he grew up at a time of immense dislocation and unrest during which both his older brothers, Patshewyah and Quiltenock, were killed. Before the age of thirty he himself had become the Half-Sun.

As a child of ten Moses spent some time at Henry H. Spalding's Protestant mission to the Nez Perce people at Lapwai, Idaho. There he acquired his white name, a knowledge of Bible stories (but not a faith in Christianity), and the ability to speak the tongue of the non-Salish Nez Perces. Soon after returning to his own people he killed his first man, a Blackfoot, while with a Salish-speaking buffalo hunting-party on the great plains east of the Rockies. So he became a man and took his first wives.

In the course of his life, Moses had a number of wives, including a Flathead woman, Quemollah, daughter of the great Yakima leader Owhi, Quemollah's sister Mary, a Wanapum girl, and Peotsenmy, a Nez Perce, and some of these marriages were arranged to cement political relationships with other Plateau peoples. Such alliances were severely tested as white incursions into the territory increased. In 1855 Moses and his elder brother Quiltenock attended the treaty conferences with Governor Stevens. It was a grasping treaty which took from the Indians a vast tract of land between the Cascades and Spokane, Lake Chelan and the Oregon border. It immediately led to bitter resentment and violence. Moses participated in raids against miners and settlers and in the defeat of the detachment of regular troops sent out to crush them under Major G. O. Haller. With Quiltenock's death during this series of hostilities Moses became head chief and Half-Sun to his people.

When the army rounded up the hostiles, including Owhi, the Yakima, his son Qualchan, and others—some of whom were not actually hostile but who nevertheless were executed—Moses became a fugitive. He avoided councils with whites for several years and, when he started to attend, took a middle position. Smohalla, the prophet of the Wanapums, advocated an absolute return to traditional Indian ways, a right relationship with the land, and no contact with whites. Spokane Garry, Lawyer of the Nez Perces and others, councilled accommodation to white ways and the adoption of Christianity. Moses is reputed to have earlier fought hand-to-hand with Smohalla and to have left him for dead. Even if that was not so, he always resisted the prophet's teachings; he accepted new white weapons, coffee and other trade goods, and he eventually came to appreciate some aspects of white education. On the other hand, he strongly resisted being moved on to a reservation and the allocation of missionaries to the people. In 1871 he addressed W. P. Winans, the Indian Agent for eastern Washington, as follows:

> You agents all say that you are sent by the superintendant and each one
> speaks differently so that my heart is divided towards you ... The Indians
> don't receive any better treatment from the whites on account of their

religion. The Indians think they do right to pray but when the whites see them assembled for worship they mock them; and treat them the same as they would a band of fast horses; they drive them off. The white man is the cause of our sorrow . . . I fear the ruin of my people is coming. Now you tell me to fence and cultivate my land . . . that the government will give me a deed for it and then it will be mine. My parents gave birth to me here, and I fancy that this is my Country . . . I don't expect always to live; but when you white and we red men die we shall have to give an account of ourselves before our Maker. Let me remain in my own Country and I shall die contented.

For the remainder of his life Moses attempted to hold to this sort of middle position, but it was to prove increasingly difficult. In 1872 the Colville Reservation was established and there was pressure on him to accept a place for his people either on it or on the Yakima Reservation. In 1877 the Nez Perce War raged and, along with Smohalla, he could so easily have joined in and led a general conflagration in the Northwest; like Smohalla, however, he restrained his people. In 1878 he led a large war-party of his men against a volunteer force under Colonel Enoch Pike which had come to destroy him or to put him on the Yakima Reservation. He succeeded in avoiding a fight with Pike and being incarcerated on the reservation. Later in the year the murder occurred of a rancher and his pregnant wife, the Perkins, by a group of Umatilla renegades whose families had been murdered by army gunboat fire. Moses would not allow them into his camps, but neither would he cooperate in bringing them under arrest. A white posse was sent to cajole him into helping with their arrest, but it eventually arrested *him*. He was jailed and bound in chains. Fortunately for Moses, the Bureau of Indian Affairs and the army were at odds about what should be done with him, and he was able to go to Washington, D.C. There he pleaded that he had consistently used force only when confronted by force and that his desire had always been for peace. The result of his diplomacy was the offer and acceptance, in 1879, of a large reservation to the east of the Cascades adjoining the Colville Reservation and extending southwards from the Canadian border to Lake Chelan.

It was precisely Moses' success which inflamed the white settlers of the Northwest against him. It also bothered some of the other Indian peoples because he was recognized by the government as official head chief of the Wenatchees, Entiats, Chelans, Methows, and, even, the Okanogans, San Poils, Nespelems and Colvilles. Moreover, he declined actually to settle on his new reservation; instead, he moved nomadically over it to his old haunts along the Columbia River and settled, if anywhere, on the Colville Reservation. And the Moses Reservation itself was coveted by cattlemen and miners; the troops camped by it did nothing, it seemed to Moses, to remove them, and the white cattle rangers were not forthcoming in granting him rent for the lands said to be leased from him. Tension mounted and, finally, in 1884, the sale of the Moses Reservation was agreed upon. Some of the proceeds were allocated to Moses' people, some to others already on the Colville Reservation, such as Tonasket's people, and some to those forced off the Moses or Columbia Reservation, such as Sarsopkin's Okanogans. In time, some of the other Indians came to feel that Moses had got the best of the deal—which certainly included a clause for an annual thousand-dollar payment to him personally— and they claimed that he had sold their land from under them.

37 Mother and children. An older resident of the Colville Reservation identified the mother as Peotsenmy. In 1893 Chief Moses took a Nez Perce woman from Lapwai, Idaho, as a secondary wife. She changed her name from Tamatsatsamy to Peotsenmy when she moved in with the Columbia chieftain, but she did not give up her land rights on the reservation in Idaho. However, when Moses died she, together with her children, elected to stay with his senior wife, Mary, until she herself died prematurely in 1902

39 *Opposite* Chief Joe Moses. Joe Moses, whose Indian name was probably Pits-ka-stoo-ya, assumed a position of prominence after Moses' death. He was a nephew of the great Chief and, as Moses had no adult surviving sons, had a claim to succeed him. In this picture the headdress he is wearing probably once belonged to Chief Moses himself (see also plate 93)

From this time until his death in 1899 Moses' influence and power waned. He was not fully welcome in the Nespelem Valley. Personal tragedies dogged his family: his heirs were killed, smallpox took off many of his children, and alcohol threatened him as much as it did some of his favorite young men. He was once even jailed as a common drunkard. He had a minor diplomatic success when his old friend Chief Joseph and his Nez Perce band were settled on the reservation and eventually chose to live in the Nespelem Valley. But the North Half of the reservation was ceded to the whites, many of the chiefs were rankled by what they saw as Moses' misplaced dominance, and white incursions increased on the South Half. To whites he became something of a pathetic figure, a joke at their celebrations, and to Indian leaders a lazy and meddlesome irritant. Nevertheless, when he died there was much lamentation: his death marked the passing of an era. And one event confirms that he was remembered as at least a symbolically important figure by whites of even the lowest, most grasping kind: five years after his death a bunch of grave robbers desecrated his burial plot to steal his watch, his beadwork, and his presidential peace medal.

Cool-Cool-a-Weela. In the early 1900s, Professor Edmond S. Meany, prominent historian of the Pacific Northwest, wrote on the back of his print of Latham's picture of Cool-Cool: "Box Canyon. Rich man. Okanogan." Cool-Cool was not a chief in any traditional sense, but was extremely influential among the Okanogans residing near him, partly because he was so wealthy. Sometimes known as Coxey (or Coxit) George, he owned many horses, the traditional unit of wealth for Plateau peoples, and took it upon himself to defend his people against white incursions. In 1892, for example, he protested strongly to the Agent about the attempt by the authorities of Okanogan County (the closest administrative unit to his part of the reservation and in which many Okanogans lived) to tax Indians on their

38 Sister and grandchild of Chief Moses

40 Cool-Cool-a-Weela is depicted here in ceremonial dress and carrying a painted eagle-wing fan

41 *Opposite above* Chief Joseph in ceremonial dress, 1903. A contemporary historian, Thomas Prosch, wrote as follows on the back of his print of this picture: "Before the Chief would pose for this picture . . . he extracted $10 from the artist"

42 *Opposite below* Bareback rider and ponies. Horses were units of wealth for Plateau peoples. The horse this man is riding is marked with the brand of Owhi, a Yakima resident on the Colville Reservation who had gone through the Nez Perce War with Chief Joseph's people

personal property. He was, in a sense, a transitional figure: although illiterate, he understood the white man's reverence for material wealth and, to some extent, shared it, while at the same time he wished to protect his people and himself from having to swim—or, as seemed more likely then, sink—in the general stream of American economic life.

Joseph. In October 1877, on a snow-driven battlefield amidst the Bear Paw Mountains of northern Montana, at the close of a bitter struggle, Chief Joseph surrendered on behalf of those Nez Perces who had refused to sign away their lands to the whites and who had, after much provocation, refused to move on to the Nez Perce Reservation in Idaho. He spoke as follows:

Tell General Howard I know his heart. What he told me before, I have it in my heart. I am tired of fighting. Our chiefs are killed. Looking Glass is dead. Toohoolhoolzote is dead. The old men are all dead. It is the young men who say, "yes" or "no". He who led the young men is dead. My people, some of them, have run away to the hills, and have no blankets, no food. No one knows where they are—perhaps freezing to death. I want to have time to look for my children, and see how many of them I can find. Maybe I shall find them among the dead. Hear me, my chiefs. I am tired. My heart is sick and sad. From where the sun now stands I will fight no more forever.

The simplicity and pathos, the force and stark beauty of the speech caught the American public imagination.

43 Chief Joseph's winter camp, c1901. This long, composite form of tepee was favored by Plateau peoples, especially the Nez Perces

The story of Nez Perce involvement with Americans, from their hospitality to members of the Lewis and Clark Expedition in 1805, through their inter-factional disputes in the face of encroaching Christianity and settlers, to their confrontations with government officials in a series of treaty councils, is a long and complex one. The episodes of the war itself were many and various, and have provided as much stirring material for students of strategy as for devotees of real-life action. The sheer scale of the war had much to do with this. It was essentially a retreat of men, women and children across over one thousand five hundred miles of some of the most extraordinary terrain—the Rocky Mountains, Yellowstone National Park, the high plains and fastnesses of northern Montana—conducted by the Nez Perces with great skill in the teeth of opposition from three armies vastly outweighing them in both men and arms. Moreover, it was a retreat which opened with victories for the Nez Perces and they never actually lost the war until the final encounter; even then, Joseph believed he was surrendering on honorable terms: the return of the Nez Perces to their "home" in peace.

As Joseph's surrender speech implies, Joseph himself was not responsible for the conduct of the war. Ollokot, Looking Glass, Poker Joe, Toohoolhoolzote, and others were the leading fighters and generals. Joseph, like the elderly White Bird, was assigned the extremely important logistical task of moving

72

the women and children out in safety at each outbreak of hostilities. But by the war's end, of the major leaders only he and White Bird remained alive, and White Bird elected to flee to Canada. Also, even before the war, Joseph was well-known for his opposition to white encroachment into his own Wallowa Valley territory. At the last council before the war he had told General Howard:

> If I thought you were sent by the Creator I might be induced to think you had a right to dispose of me. Do not misunderstand me, but understand me fully with reference to my affection for the land. I never said the land was mine to do with as I chose. The one who has a right to dispose of it is the one who has created it. I claim a right to live on my land, and accord you the privilege to live on yours.

Thus, it is perhaps not surprising that the war itself came to be thought of as Joseph's own special vendetta; General Howard titled his account of it, published in 1881, as follows: *Nez Perce Joseph, an account of his ancestors, his lands, his confederates, his enemies, his murders, his war, his pursuit and capture.*

In fact, in the years of suffering after the war Joseph came into his own, though as a tragic figure. For the rest of his life he waged a constant political battle, of varying degrees of intensity, to try to get his own band and himself resettled in the Wallowa, the ancestral home of his own father, Tu-eka-kas or Old Joseph. He never succeeded, but in his efforts to do so he emerged as an eloquent spokesman for the ideals of liberty, fraternity and equality upon which the constitution of the United States itself is assumed to rest.

After the surrender in Montana, despite the misgivings of Colonel (later General) Nelson A. Miles, the actual victor at the Bear Paws Battle, the captured Nez Perces were transported to Indian Territory. Dumped in insanitary camps far from the mountains and streams of their own Northwest, they died rapidly. In 1879 Joseph and Yellow Bull were allowed to go to Washington, D.C., to put their case. In *The North American Review* for April 1879 there appeared Joseph's "An Indian's View of Indian Affairs", which says in part:

> I have carried a heavy load on my back ever since I was a boy. I learned then that we were but few, while the white men were many, and that we could not hold our own with them. We were like deer. They were like grizzly bears. We had a small country. Their country was large. We were contented to let things remain as the Great Spirit Chief made them. They were not; and would change the rivers and mountains if they did not suit them ...
>
> If the white man wants to live in peace with the Indian he can live in peace. There need be no trouble. Treat all men alike. Give them all the same law. Give them all an even chance to live and grow. All men were made by the same Great Spirit Chief. They are all brothers. The earth is the Mother of all people, and all people should have equal rights upon it. You might as well expect the rivers to run backward as that any man who was born a free man should be contented penned up and denied liberty to go where he pleases. If you tie a horse to a stake, do you expect he will grow fat? If you pen an Indian up on a small spot of earth, and compel him to stay there, he will not be contented—nor will he grow and prosper. I have asked some of the great white chiefs where they get their authority to say to the Indian

that he shall stay in one place, while he sees white men going where they please. They cannot tell me.

I only ask of the Government to be treated as all other men are treated. If I cannot go to my own home, let me have a home in some country where my people will not die so fast. I would like to go to Bitter Root Valley. There my people would be healthy; where they are now they are dying. Three have died since I left my camp to come to Washington ...

Whenever the white man treats the Indian as they treat each other, then we shall have no more wars. We shall be all alike—brothers of one father and mother, with one sky above and one country around us, and one government for all. Then the Great Spirit Chief who rules above will smile upon this land, and send rain to wash out the bloody spots made by brothers' hands upon the face of the earth. For this time the Indian race are waiting and praying. I hope that no more groans of wounded men and women will ever go to the ear of the Great Spirit Chief above, and that all people may be one people.

In-mut-too-yah-lat-lat has spoken for his people.

Young Joseph

Many more Nez Perces had to die before they were allowed to return to the Northwest in 1885. Some, mostly the Christians, were allowed to settle on the Nez Perce Reservation in Idaho with those Nez Perces who had not gone to war, but Joseph's band was exiled to the Colville Reservation. They were not truly welcomed there and Joseph himself was treated as a malign influence by a succession of Agents; he was constantly reported on, his movements were curtailed, and he was frequently demeaned.

But he did not give up the fight. In 1900 he succeeded in reopening the case, only to have Indian Inspector James McLaughlin promptly find against him. In 1903 he delivered speeches in Seattle, and as late as 1904, the year of his death, he was still pressing the issue in Washington, D.C., in New York, and at the St Louis Exposition.

In white terms it might seem a matter for wonder that a man with no known formal "civilized" education, who was probably born in a cave on Joseph Creek, Oregon, in 1840, could so forcefully express the ideals now accepted as axiomatic by believers in democracy. But, like all traditionally educated Nez Perces, Joseph had only to look to the earth. In 1911 Edward S. Curtis wrote in the eighth volume of his *The North American Indian*, "Indians in general are indeed close to nature, but the individual Nez Perce with his interwoven devotional system, communed with almost unlimited nature." Smohalla, prophet of the dreamers, who reaffirmed the traditional Indian reverence for nature, had expressed very poetically their religious feelings about the earth when he explained why his young men could not work. Joseph himself put it more coolly and stressed the implicit moral imperative: "The earth and myself are of one mind. The measure of the land and the measure of our bodies are the same." In his last years at Nespelem he must often have wondered if such natural justice was ever to be had.

Yellow Bull (Chuslum Mox-mox), sometimes known as Weyatanatoo Wahy-akt or Sun Necklace, was born about 1830 into an old warrior family in that Nez Perce territory on the Salmon River which fell under the leadership of Chief White Bird. White Bird was one of the Nez Perce leaders who most

strongly opposed making any concessions to whites. Also, as white incursions increased during the 1860s and 1870s, White Bird's band seemed to suffer disproportionately from random acts of violence or contempt perpetrated on Indians by insecure and aggressive new settlers. There was extremely high tension just before those Nez Perce who had always refused to sign away their lands were due, under threat of military action, to enter the Nez Perce Reservation in Idaho. It was released when a group of young men from White Bird's band murdered some whites who had earlier insulted and ill-treated them. These acts of violence triggered the Nez Perce War of 1877. A leader of the small war-party of young men who killed the whites was Sarpsis Ilp-pilp or Red Moccasin Tops, Yellow Bull's favorite son.

45 Chief David Williams, c1903

The first engagement of the war proper, the White Bird Battle, fought on June 17, 1877, occurred when Captain David Perry ignored a flag of truce sent out by Joseph and other Nez Perce leaders. In the fight which followed, Yellow Bull, though already middle-aged, distinguished himself. Sarpsis Ilp-pilp was one of three warriors to fight as a unit; they wore red coats made of woollen blankets which had been given to them by Yellow Bull, and each became renowned for his bravery. But the war was to prove tragic for Yellow Bull. In the Big Hole Battle, when the Nez Perces were surprised in their camp at dawn by a large force under General John Gibbon, Sarpsis Ilp-pilp was shot through the throat and killed. Several younger warriors, including Yellow Wolf, vied with each other to recover his body for Yellow Bull to bury and his sacred wolfskin to wear. The Chief buried his son in a shallow grave among the rocks.

In the final combat of the war, just forty miles from Canada and freedom, the Nez Perce camp was charged by Colonel Miles' army and the Bear Paws Battle was started. It was the beginning of October and a snowstorm from the north also attacked the half-starved and exhausted Indian families. Some of the best fighting men were lost. Under a flag of truce Miles called for talks with Joseph, who readily complied; when he refused to surrender, however, Miles, in violation of the truce, detained Joseph in his camp, tied in blankets and quartered among the mules. In retaliation Yellow Bull ordered the holding of Lieutenant Lovell H. Jerome in the Nez Perce camp. Two days later Joseph and Jerome were exchanged at a spot marked by a buffalo robe upon the ground. The fighting continued, but the destruction was so great, especially of women and children, that when General Howard and Colonel Miles offered the Nez Perces a peaceful return to their homes in the Northwest if they surrendered, the leaders agreed and Joseph surrendered.

When this was done, White Bird and many of his band escaped during the night and headed for Canada. Yellow Bull, although one of White Bird's people, elected to abide by Joseph's surrender. The Nez Perces were not, however, returned to the Northwest, but were transported to Fort Leavenworth, Kansas, and thence to Indian Territory. Many died of malaria and other sicknesses. When Chief Joseph was allowed to plead the Nez Perce cause in Washington, D.C., in 1879, the other leader to accompany him was Yellow Bull.

When they were finally allowed to return to the Northwest in 1885 they were simply dumped for a year in haphazard camps near the Agency headquarters. Joseph and the majority elected to move to the Nespelem Valley, while Yellow Bull and sixteen survivors of his own people decided to stay at the Agency. A few years later he and his people took up allotments of

land on the Nez Perce Reservation in Idaho. His friendship for Joseph, however, was unimpaired; during the 1890s he visited the Nespelem Nez Perces several times. Thus it was appropriate that Yellow Bull was the most senior of all the surviving non-treaty Nez Perces after Joseph's death in 1904.

In June 1905, though considerably aged and blind, he journeyed to Nespelem to deliver an oration at the erection of a monument at Joseph's new grave. He spoke of the universality of grief and respect for Joseph that the presence of both white and red men at Joseph's tomb signified and said that Joseph's words would survive as long as the monument. A few days later he delivered from horseback a longer and more stirring speech to the Nez Perces gathered for Joseph's potlatch, the giving away of the old Chief's possessions. While his horse circled the tepee three times, his words so moved the people that the women covered their faces with their hair and wailed as he passed.

David Williams was known in his youth as Eelahweemah or About Sleep. He was approximately twelve years old when the Nez Perce War broke out. His father was a member of Joseph's Wallowa Valley Nez Perces and the family was related by marriage to that of Yellow Bull. At first the war meant excitement for the growing boy; he and other boys carried drinking water to the Indians at the forward positions who were exchanging shots with the white soldiers. But, as for so many others, the Big Hole Battle was the turning point: the troops fired into his father's tepee at dawn, people were wounded and when they sought shelter in a shallow gully—two children and five women—his mother was shot dead next to him. Later, after the surrender, his baby brother died of malaria on the southern plains.

When Joseph's Nez Perces came to settle at Nespelem David Williams was a man. Despite an illness which deprived him of the sight of one eye, he came to be respected not only by his own people, but by other tribes on the reservation and, ultimately, by whites. Very early on he firmly decided to make the best of their situation and not to think of ever returning to the Wallowa Valley, whatever the hopes of others might be. To this end he seems to have tried to get to know the Nespelems, the original inhabitants of the valley, and to have gained their confidence. By the time the celebrations were held at Chief Joseph's reburial, he was able to act as an interpreter between the Nez Perces and the Salish-speaking Nespelems. On the other hand, he was intensely loyal to Joseph and to the tenets of traditional Nez Perce life. He took his place on ceremonial occasions and preferred Indian dress.

When Joseph died, David Williams was considered by many to be suitable to succeed him as chief, but Albert Waters was chosen. Not long afterwards, however, Williams did become chief of the Nespelem Nez Perces and held the position until his death in 1920.

Annie from Wenatchee. Several older inhabitants of the Colville Reservation identified the subject of two of Latham's finest portraits (see plates 48 and 85) as Annie, and they claimed she came from Wenatchee. The environs of Wenatchee, now irrigated from semi-desert into a region of abundant apple production, were once home to a small group of Salish-speaking people; as they became dispossessed some moved to the Colville Reservation and there continued an age-old pattern of inter-marriage with members of the various small Plateau tribes. Here certainty ends and guesswork begins. Annie is thought to have been married to a Nez Perce known to the whites as Robert Johnson. At some time around the turn of the century Johnson had a wife

named Peo-na-nikt, a Nez Perce, but his name does appear on an Agency payroll as a day laborer in 1897 and the name recorded as his wife's at that time is Minnie, possibly designating the same person as Annie. Such confusions as this apply to more than the simple identification of the subjects of photographic portraits: it is presented here because it gives a little insight into a great need for and the difficulties encountered in recovering the history of average Indian individuals. Of Indian chiefs and notables little enough is known, of ordinary people—almost nothing. And in a few years no one at all will remain who might, conceivably, remember Annie, or Minnie. Indeed, to document the life story of the pattern on her Pendleton blanket would probably be easier than to do much beyond pointing to the bare records which testify to *her* existence.

Charlie Wilpocken appeared on the Agency payroll in 1897 as a day laborer. He seems to have started two years earlier as a replacement for Owhi, a Yakima Indian who had gone through the Nez Perce War with Joseph's band and settled with them near Nespelem. Owhi left the job claiming the government overseer at the sawmill overworked him. It would appear from this that Charlie Wilpocken would have been a more pliable figure. But this was not so. In fact, he strongly resisted white influences, despite living quite close to Latham and other whites at Nespelem. He wore his hair long and always dressed for ceremonial occasions and took a traditional stance, even so far as threatening to kill an Indian from Moses' tribe who had destroyed a Nez Perce-owned horse. He lived well into the twentieth century and is still remembered today by some reservation residents, both as a joker and as a traditionalist.

Alice Yellow Wolf was a daughter of Yellow Wolf, one of the longest surviving non-treaty Nez Perces; he lived to be nearly eighty, dying in 1935. Yellow Wolf was related to Chief Joseph and, in fact, was living in Joseph's tepees at the beginning and through the Nez Perce War. The events of Yellow Wolf's life have been immortalized in a classic account compiled by Lucullus Virgil McWhorter. McWhorter came to know Yellow Wolf when the latter camped on his ranch in the Yakima Valley in 1908 and from then until Yellow Wolf's death he collected information, especially on a field trip through the whole country of the war; the result was *Yellow Wolf: His Own Story*. The book tells much about Yellow Wolf the man and fighter and relates episodes of the war with graphic detail, including Yellow Wolf's capture of white tourists in the Yellowstone National Park. It tells of the defeat and Yellow Wolf's decision to flee with White Bird's band to Sitting Bull's Sioux people in Canada, and of his long wanderings before getting back to the Nez Perce Reservation in Idaho, his subsequent incarceration in Indian Territory, and his final release to Nespelem. But it says very little about his family. Alice was most likely born at Nespelem—and that is about all that can be surmised. On the back of his print of Latham's portrait Professor Meany wrote, "Alice, daughter of Yellow Wolf", and such has become her primary identity.

Chica-ma-poo, or Old Jean. On the back of a Latham picture of Chica-ma-poo, Meany wrote in about 1901: "Oldest surviving Nez Perce at Nespelem. Fought like a brave in the 1877 war." She herself, though born in the early days of American-Nez Perce contact, made much more modest claims for herself when, through the agency of a former Indian Service

49 Charlie Wilpocken

50 *Opposite* Charlie
Wilpocken and family. One
older present-day resident of
the Colville Reservation has
identified the woman as
Wilpocken's second wife,
Kil-ess-tum, a Yakima

51 Two of Charlie
Wilpocken's sons. The older
child is Art Cercle, who lived
until the early 1970s, while
the younger one died of
stomach burns in childhood.
Art Cercle is also depicted in

plate 5. Between the two
boys is an otter skin decorated
with mirrors; these were
prized forms of adornment,
especially during dances

52 Alice, daughter of Yellow Wolf

53 *Opposite* A woman and two girls, June 1905. The woman is Annie Yellow Wolf, a wife of Yellow Wolf. The girl on the left is Annie Sam (who also appears in plate 20) and the one on the right is Mary Tom, a Colville who was half-sister to Annie Yellow Wolf

employee who knew Nez Perce, Henry M. Steele, she briefly recorded her life story in December 1901. Steele, like us all, was heir to the clichés, turns of phrase, and tones of voice of his time, and used such expressions as "happy hunting grounds" to evoke the idea of an Indian heaven. The following record, never previously published, approaches as closely as it is possible for us to come—despite the manner of its telling—to an elderly Nez Perce woman's summation of her life's experience as she saw it at the turn of the century:

My Indian name is So-ko-mop-o and the name given to me by the white people is Jean. I was born in the territory now embraced in the State of Idaho, about thirty miles from the present site of Asotin, Washington, by a small stream called by my people A-la-hah. This stream enters into the Snake River. As near as I am able to remember, I am ninety years old and perhaps more. My father's name was Che-in-wa-hiah, a full blooded Nez Perce. My mother's name was So-ko-mop-o and she was a full blooded Walla Walla. I was named after my mother. I spent my childhood with my parents pursuing all the pleasures and pastimes of Indian life, hunting, fishing, and gathering roots. I love to think of my young life, it was so happy and gay. When I was about eighteen years old, I was married to my first husband, whose name was Tom-ya-nun. He was a Nez Perce brave, handsome and kind. I cannot say how long I lived with him but seven children was the result of our union, five boys and two girls. They are all, now, dead, and are buried in different parts of Idaho. I hope to visit their graves once more before I die. My first husband died. After being a widow for five years, I married Skom-chits-ka-nun, a Nez Perce who was wealthy and owned large herds of cattle and horses. The result of this union was two children, one boy and one girl. The girl has long since died and my son is still living at Nespelem, Washington, and is a member of Chief Joseph's band. My son's name is In-mat-hia-hia and he is the only living child out of a family of nine children. When Joseph and our people concluded to fight for his forefather's birthright, I was anxious to join him, but my husband protested against my engaging in hostilities against the whites. Regardless of his entreaties and objections, I joined Allocott and Joseph and went all through the campaign. I left my home and my husband to assist in the struggle, caused by the encroachment of the whites. To go into details of this long and bitter fight would take much time and resurrect many unpleasant memories. During Joseph's march I often wept in sorrow and shed bitter tears in witnessing the wanton murder of so many of my relations and friends. We often hid in the underbrush and willows to screen ourselves from the musketry of the white soldiers. After such engagements the men would come and tell us who had been slain in battle. Sometimes they would bring in the mangled form of one of our braves whose life was slowly ebbing away. We always cared for the wounded as best we could until death claimed its victim. We generally buried the bodies among the rocks and in secret places. We did this so the soldiers would not know how many had been killed. After the capture and surrender of Joseph, I left and lived with the Sioux Indians. When Joseph returned from Indian Territory, I joined him at Lapwai, Idaho. In the meantime, my husband had died and his bands of horses and cattle, with other property, had entirely vanished, having been managed by unscrupulous Indians and bad white men. Many years of my life have been filled with sadness. Death has swept away my

children and my two husbands and we have suffered great injustice from the government. It has taken away my old home and declines to allow me to spend the few years that I may live, in the beautiful country where I was born and spent much of my younger life. Little mounds mark the resting places of my children and naturally I would like to be laid at rest there myself. I am now held as a captive and fed as a common prisoner, and for what reason I cannot understand. I have nothing to live for, my Indian pride has been crushed out of me and I fully realize my keen humiliation. I am a member of no church, I belong to no creed, but I think when I die the Great Father beyond the clouds will be kind and just to me. I believe I will meet my husbands and children, also my departed friends, in the happy hunting grounds, and what a happy reunion that will be. I bear no malice or hatred toward any one and feel kindly toward all. I am an aunt of Chief Joseph and I think him a brave, honest and fearless man who fought against overwhelming odds for the defence of his home and people.

Indian names have been recorded in different ways by the various whites who have transcribed them; hence Meany's Chica-ma-poo compared with Steele's So-ko-mop-o. Steele's transcriptions are not notably inaccurate, though they do deviate from some commonly accepted forms; for example, for Joseph's brother he gives Allocott rather than the more usual Ollokot (Frog). But it is worth pointing out that Lucullus Virgil McWhorter, the indefatiguable chronicler of Nez Perce history, has offered spellings for some of the names Old Jean mentions which differ just slightly from Steele's versions and which help to clarify her family relationships. McWhorter has See-kum-ses-Kun-nin (Horse Blanket), which probably denotes the same person as Steele's Skom-chits-ka-nun, Old Jean's second husband, father of her only surviving son. Steele gives that son's name as In-mat-hia-hia, and this

55 Peo-peo Tholekt, June 1905. Peo-peo's magnificent headdress of eagle feathers is the same one as that worn by Yellow Bull when he came to deliver his oration at Chief Joseph's reburial (see plate 44)

most likely refers to the same individual as McWhorter's Hein-mot Hih-hih (White Thunder or White Lightning). Such a person was living at Nespelem in 1901 and of his several names the one most commonly used as He-mene Mox-mox or Yellow Wolf. As was noted in the sketch of Alice, daughter of Yellow Wolf, McWhorter recorded this prominent warrior's tale in *Yellow Wolf: His Own Story*, a classic account of Indian pride and modesty, physical bravery and spirituality. The events of Yellow Wolf's memories tally with those of Old Jean's reminiscences. Yellow Wolf remembered that his mother certainly did fight as well as a man during the 1877 war: "My mother could use the gun against soldiers if they bothered her," he said. "She could ride any wild horse and shoot straight. She could shoot the buffalo and was not afraid of the grizzly bear." Clearly, Chica-ma-poo was the honored mother of an

56 Lizzie Cayuse, *c*1903

honored son. Yellow Wolf's name for her was Yi-yik Wa-sum-wah. Swan Woman.

Peo-peo Tholekt, whose name means Bird Alighting, was a young warrior, newly married, when the Nez Perce War broke out. He was a member of Chief Looking Glass' band. At first this band opted for peace. However, when the troops came and shot up their village, Looking Glass took up the rifle. According to Peo-peo's friend Yellow Wolf, it was Peo-peo's quickness in wresting a gun from a white soldier at the Big Hole Battle that enabled another warrior, Lakochets Kunnin, to kill the soldier in hand-to-hand combat. Later in the same battle he was with Sarpsis Ilp-pilp when he was killed. Also, he buried part of a captured cannon so that it could not be used against the Nez Perces if recovered. Despite several narrow escapes, he survived the war intact and eventually took up an allotment on the Nez Perce Reservation in Idaho.

In his later years, Peo-peo Tholekt developed into something of a politician. On the Nez Perce Reservation in Idaho he became influential among the non-Christians and many, both non-Christian and Christian, believed that he was hoping to inherit Chief Joseph's mantle as leader of the traditionalist faction. Some went so far as to view him as a "schemer". Peo-peo did maintain close links with Joseph, but when the Chief died Peo-peo's claims to his eagle headdress went unheeded. Although he came to Nespelem for the potlatch held after Joseph's reburial, he returned to Lapwai unhonored. Several times during the period from 1910 to 1930 he joined with others to try to get Chief Joseph's body reburied once again under a better monument, first in the Wallowa Valley, then on the reservation in Idaho. However, such attempts were seen as covert bids for power and always opposed by the Nespelem Nez Perces, so he failed.

Lizzie Cayuse, as her name indicates, was a member of the Cayuse family, a prominent non-treaty Nez Perce family at Nespelem. It is likely that her grandfather was a son of Cayuse Woman, second wife of Chief Joseph's father and a member of the Cayuse tribe. She was considered beautiful; on his print of Latham's portrait of her Meany wrote " 'belle' of the Nez Perce".

In January 1904 S. M. McCowan, Assistant Chief of the Department of Anthropology for the St Louis Exposition of 1904, wrote to the Agent for the Colville Reservation asking him to send Joseph to the exposition "as one of the representative old Indians for our Indian Exhibit ...", saying that these "old time Indians" would be contrasted "with the younger generation attending government schools". (McCowan added a postscript: "I presume he can be kept on good behavior during such attendance.") Whether Lizzie Cayuse attended a government school is doubtful, but she was certainly chosen to accompany her chief to the Exposition.

And there were others, people who were just names on an allotment roll, or who were not even names; people who left no record of their existence at all, except, possibly, the mound of an unmarked grave in one of the burial plots which increasingly dotted the reservation. Traditionally, most Plateau peoples buried their dead with the corpse in a flexed position on its side, and wrapped in a woven mat. A thin pole was planted at the head of the grave. Items significant to the dead one were often attached to the pole: eagle feathers, a beaded bag, or little bells which would tinkle when the wind agitated the enduring earth.

3 The Physician Photographer
"A superannuated gentleman"

Dr Latham, a pioneer in the Pacific Northwest at the end of the nineteenth century, was himself, like so many other early settlers in eastern Washington, born into a pioneer family in the Middle West. He was the son of a prominent early resident of Columbus, Ohio, Bela Latham. Bela Latham came from Vermont, was postmaster in Columbus from 1829 to 1841, a director of the Clinton Bank by 1834, and a prominent Freemason. Edward Hempstead Latham was born in 1845, the sixth of seven children. He was only three when his father died in 1848 and although he, most of his brothers and sisters, and his mother, Rosanna, continued to live in Columbus, his uncle, Allen Latham, became his official guardian. It is likely that during his later childhood and young manhood Edward spent considerable periods of time in his uncle's home, probably in Kentucky, and certainly by the time the Civil War was well under way, in 1862, his name no longer appeared in the Columbus city directory. His mother probably died there during his teenage years, the mid-1860s. The Latham family appears to have scattered. Edward's younger brother Frank went West. By the time Edward came to visit him in 1892, some thirty years after their parting, he was Land Agent for the North Pacific Coast Railroad in San Francisco, and responsible for buying up huge tracts of land on the California coast for railroad and property development.

Nothing is known of Edward's early manhood—what his first profession was, for instance, or whether or not he enlisted for service at the tail end of the Civil War—but he was certainly married on July 28, 1870 to Mary Archer, daughter of a pioneer settler in New Richmond, Ohio. The Lathams had three sons during the 1870s, Frank, James and Warren. Edward and Mary must have been gifted with extraordinary energy because, as well as raising these boys, in 1882 Edward graduated in pharmacy from the Cincinnati College of Pharmacy, Ohio; in 1884 he was granted a degree in medicine by Miami Medical College, Cincinnati, and in 1886 Mary graduated in medicine from the Cincinnati College of Medicine and Surgery. As a medical student Mary Latham was one of the first class of women to be admitted to the clinical wards of Cincinnati General Hospital: this is, perhaps, the first evidence of the ambition and dedication which were to take her to the top of her profession.

The Lathams set up a joint practice in Cincinnati, but Mary was delicate in health and needed a drier air than the riverside city of Cincinnati could provide, so in 1887 they sought the more salubrious climate of Spokane Falls, Washington. Spokane Falls was a large pioneer village then, with muddy streets in winter and dust in summer—barely a town; but it was expanding rapidly and within a year or so became the thrusting city of Spokane, with street cars, plate glass in the large store windows and a big depot for the Great Northern Railroad. The Lathams set up practice in the same downtown

57 Dr Latham and a
companion, by Frank F.
Avery. Latham is seated

building and very quickly established themselves as a prominent professional couple.

It seems that thereafter Mary prospered, and Edward did not. She became famous almost overnight, especially as an expert on the ailments of women and children. She was elected Chairman of the Medical Department of the Washington Branch of the Queen Isabella Association and in that role represented the State of Washington at the Chicago World's Fair Columbian Exposition of 1893. She was involved in numerous community activities, including the founding of a public library for the growing city. Also, she acquired land for development in Spokane and for ranching in Palouse County, she started to write feature articles for a number of magazines, and she had mining interests. For a time she was probably the most prominent woman physician in the Pacific Northwest. Meanwhile, her husband busied himself with his hobby, photography, quietly practised his profession, and, it seems, drank quite heavily.

In January 1890 Edward was appointed Agency Physician on the Colville Reservation, with single man's quarters at the Nespelem sub-Agency, over a hundred miles from Spokane by wagon road. The Lathams drifted apart and were divorced by 1900. Mary died in 1917.

The *Annual Report of the Commissioner for Indian Affairs* of 1889 speaks of the life of a physician on a reservation "with poor accommodations, small salary, and few of the modern appliances and help" as "dreary enough to all except to him who realizes the noble part he may perform in helping to lift this people out of superstitious regard for the grotesque need of the 'medicine man'." The list of qualities and duties expected of a physician by the Bureau of Indian Affairs is worth quoting at some length because it will enable today's reader to appreciate more fully the degree to which Latham's own views and actions were typical of this branch of government—and, indeed, of the general culture of the time—as well as the degree to which he fell short of, or exceeded, such general expectations.

SYNOPSIS OF QUALIFICATIONS AND DUTIES OF AGENCY PHYSICIANS.

To be eligible to the position of agency physician the applicant ought to have a good general education, must be a regular graduate of some reputable medical college, and be actually engaged in the practice of medicine. He must be between twenty-five and forty-five years of age, temperate, active, industrious, in sound health, and must possess a good personal and professional character. The application for appointment must be made upon blanks provided for the purpose, which will be furnished upon request. A copy of the applicant's diploma and of his licence to practise medicine must be filed at the same time. Married men are preferred to those who are single.

Attending to private practice or other business outside of the agency is prohibited, as it leads to endless complaints and opens the door for neglect of official duties. The physician must devote his entire time and professional skill to the Indians and agency employés.

He should at all times strive to overcome the evil influence of the native "medicine men," to abolish their superstitious rites and barbarous customs, to gain the respect and confidence of the Indians, and to extend his influence among them by kind treatment, exemplary habits, and prompt attention to the cases requiring medical assistance. He should be governed by the highest code of professional conduct.

The agency physician is required not only to attend to those who call upon him at his office, but also to visit the Indians at their homes, and, in addition to prescribing and administering needed medicines, to do his utmost to educate and instruct them in proper methods of living, and of caring for health.

He should exercise special care in regard to the sanitary condition of the agency and schools, and promptly report to the agent any condition, either of building or grounds, liable to cause sickness, in order that proper steps may be taken to remedy the evil.

The physician is required to make regular visits to the Indian schools, and

58 Dr Latham's quarters in
winter

during such visits he should give short talks to the pupils on the elementary principles of physiology and hygiene, explaining in a plain and simple manner the processes of digestion and the assimilation of food, the circulation of the blood, the functions of the skin, etc., by which they may understand the necessity for proper habits of eating and drinking, for cleanliness, ventilation, and other hygienic conditions. The correct manner of treating emergency cases, such as dangerous hemorrhage, syncope, prostration from heat, etc., should also be explained.

Classes should be formed composed of the most advanced and intelligent pupils, for special instruction by the physician in regard to nursing and caring for the sick, administering medicines, and preparing food for invalids, and any other points of like character on which it would be proper to give such pupils instruction.

A full statement of what the physician has done in the directions above noted should accompany his monthly report.

Monthly reports must be made to this office upon blanks furnished for the purpose, showing the number of cases and the nature of the diseases treated, care being taken to note that all the footings are correctly made, that the reports are prepared in a neat, legible manner, that all the cases appearing as treated are properly accounted for, and that the cases remaining under treatment at the end of each month are properly carried forward to the report for the succeeding month. Indian sanitary statistics should be full, accurate, and absolutely reliable.

In connection with the monthly sanitary report the physician must, from time to time, note the progress which the Indians are making toward abandoning their medicine men and adopting rational methods of treating and nursing the sick. Special attention should be given to the matter of hospitals.

The agent, being a bonded officer, is responsible under his bond for all medical supplies at his agency, and the physician must exercise prudence and sound judgment in expending such supplies. At the end of each quarter a report of medical property must be made on the proper blanks and be handed to the agent to be forwarded with his accounts to this office.

Harmony is essential to the proper conduct of an agency, and the physician, though appointed directly by this office, must treat the agent with proper respect, promptly and cheerfully obeying all orders issued by him.

So, in the iciness of January 1890, the coldest winter on record there, Latham took up residence at Nespelem. He was the first permanent white doctor and, like Joseph Bouska, the sawyer and miller, he was one of the first five or six whites of any sort to live and work there. The first year seems to have passed comparatively smoothly, but the following winter was tough, though not because of cold: on March 14, 1891 he wrote from Nespelem to the Agent, Hal J. Cole, who was at the Agency itself on the southeast edge of the reservation:

We are having hard times on the Nespilem, an epidemic of La Grip started here about the first of this month and the Indians are all sick. there have been five or six deaths so far and there are others that can hardly recover. their Medicine men have got frightened and two of them refuse to practice . . . Mr Boske has rendered me great assistance. I do not know how I should get along without his aid for my knowledge of Chinook is so limited that I cannot make them understand. Mr B is feeling badly this morning but I think and hope it is nothing serious, and that he will not be taken down, we had a hard day yesterday as we visited over fifty sick, at Snawtonic's camp

59 Nespelem. This photograph must have been taken in the early 1900s. The general store on the left is probably the one which was opened in the late 1890s to supply white miners prospecting on the reservation. On its roof is a post office sign, and the post office was opened in 1899. To the right is the hotel. This was operated for many years by Henry M. Steele, a former Indian Service employee who was especially friendly towards the Nez Perces

60 Group portrait, c1903.
Like so many of these
pictures, this group was taken
outside Latham's own house.
Charlie Wilpocken stands in
the center

we found twenty five down, at Joseph's we found thirteen and there were others we did not see, at blind Louie's camp there are fifteen or twenty sick. Owhi is down and four others at his house. Moses has lost his daughter and is sick himself but is improving. and so it is everywhere, there is not a place but some are down, so unless it is actually necessary I will not attempt to come to the agency to invoice the stock of medicine until things get in better shape here . . .

La Grippe or influenza was obviously not an everyday occurrence; nevertheless, there were always problems. Some of these were of a bureaucratic nature: the files of Agency correspondence contain hundreds of requests from Latham for order blanks so that he could order medicines; as medicines could not be issued except in response to an official blank, so the circle of inefficiency could not be broken, and the doctor's energies were expended on paperwork. Each physician also had to report regularly to his Agent and, while this must have been extremely tedious, the resulting reports now make fascinating reading. One of Latham's submissions, that for the 1891–2 financial year, was actually published in the *Annual Report of the Commissioner for Indian Affairs* for 1892:

REPORT OF PHYSICIAN AT COLVILLE AGENCY.

Nespelim, Colville Reservation, Wash., July 15, 1892.

Sir: I have the honor to present you herewith an annual report for the fiscal year ending June 30, 1892. At the beginning of this report I can think of no better subject than to describe in a few brief words the country and the different tribes of Indians I am expected to look after and treat.

My office is located in the beautiful valley of Nespelim, and the territory directly under my charge extends from the mouth of the Okanogan River at the southwest corner of the reservation, along the Columbia River to the mouth of the Sanpuell, a distance of about 70 miles, and from the Columbia back into the interior from 20 to 30 miles. In this territory there reside 800 or 900 people, consisting of a few of the Okanagan tribe, Joseph's band of Nez Perces, Moses' band of Columbias, the Nespelim and Sanpuell tribes. Indirectly, and subject to the call of the people and order of the agent, my territory extends from the mouth of the Sanpuell River up the Columbia River to the British line, a distance of 150 miles, and as much as 50 miles into the interior. This country is occupied below the Kettle River by the Colville tribe, and above the Kettle River to the British line by the Lake tribe, numbering 600 or 700. Besides all this vast territory, I have indirectly under my charge the entire Spokane Reservation, occupied by the Lower Spokanes, numbering 400 or more. In all I have between 800 and 2,000 people to look after, who are scattered over a distance of 300 miles.

I have no complaints to make. I am ready and willing at all times to respond to the calls of the Indians, and I feel sure you will support me, when I state that I have done all within my power to alleviate the suffering of these poor people. Yet I feel and know that I am not doing them justice. Should I spend my entire time in riding over this vast territory, I could not possibly make more than seven or eight trips during the year. This would require at least four good horses, two saddle horses, and two pack horses; and the actual necessary traveling expenses would amount to at least one-half the pay of a physician.

I have written the above to show in a brief manner the great need of at least one more physician to look after these people. There are buildings already erected at the agency headquarters for a physician, and after deducting the necessary traveling expenses of one physician, the additional expense to the Government would be but a trifle.

The moral and sanitary condition of the different tribes.—The few of the *Okanagans* located on the Okanagan River near its mouth, who come directly under my charge, are well advanced in civilization. They are mostly all Catholics, and are very much devoted to their religion. Their moral condition is good and their sanitary condition is also good. They are willing at all times to take the advice of the physician, and try to follow his directions. They mostly have good log houses and seem to take pride in keeping them neat and clean. They all wear citizens' clothes, and the males all have short hair. They take quite an interest in the school, and their little ones, as a rule, are very polite.

The *Nespelims* are mostly located in the Nespelim Valley and surrounding mountains. They are a peculiar class of Indians, having a religion of their own. They, as a rule, will receive no aid from the Government. They are very industrious, living in fairly good houses; and their moral and sanitary condition is good. Yet they are hard to become acquainted with. Still, with kind treatment and patience, I am happy to be able to state that I have succeeded in gaining their confidence, and now they are all my friends. To use their own language, I am their "tillicum," which means the same as brother. One case connected with these people, which has been one of great interest to me and by means of which I have gained their gratitude and confidence, I will relate:

Quil-quil-toch-in, a few years since, while hunting deer in the mountains, was pierced in the right eye by a sharp thorn, from which he suffered greatly, and finally lost the eye entirely. Last August, while he was again hunting deer, he was pierced in the left eye by a thorn. While on one of my trips through the mountains I came upon a small tent. I stopped and entering found this man suffering the most intense agony. He related the circumstances to me. I examined the eye carefully, finding it in a terrible condition. The eye had the appearance of a mass of blood. He could see nothing, and was very despondent, saying he would much rather die than lose his sight. I wanted to take him home with me, promising to do all I could for him. But no, he said he had no money to pay me. I went to his friends and talked two days with him and them, but it was always the same answer. He could not pay for the services rendered. I tried all means to persuasion I could think of, even threatening to arrest him, but to no avail. Finally I promised to use my own medicine, and persuading him he could pay me when he got well by acting as guide in the mountains, which would be the same to me as money. Finally he consented to this. I took him to my office, where for two weeks I watched over him both night and day. We were fortunate enough to have a supply of ice, and I had among my own medicines a supply of pure hydrochlorate of cocaine. It was a hard fight for two weeks. During this period all I could possibly do was to keep the inflammation from increasing. At the expiration of this time improvement set in, and from that time on he gained rapidly. The eye finally got well with a cloudy appearance, which has gradually been disappearing, and a short time since he borrowed my gun, saying he thought his sight was restored enough to shoot. He went to the mountains, and the next day returned with two fine deer, I think the happiest man I ever saw. Since that time these people have called on me a number of times.

The *Sanpuell* Indians are the worst people that I have anything to do with. They reside mostly on the Sanpuell River. They are surly, ignorant, and filthy, cultivating little land and living almost entirely by fishing and hunting. They have the same religious prejudice as the Nespelims about receiving aid from the Government. As to their morals I can not say. Their sanitary condition is not good.

Moses' Band of *Columbias.*—These people reside mostly in the Nespelim valley and surrounding mountains. They are true, genuine Indians in every sense of the word. Still they are very easy to get along with, and very pleasant if kindly treated. Old Chief Moses is very much of a gentleman. During the past year he has had good health, with the exception of trouble in one eye, which I will relate further on. As a class I think these people are the most robust and healthy Indians on either reservation. They seem to be more free from consumption, scrofula, and syphilis than any of the other tribes. Some of them have good houses, and most all of them have farms, cultivating small tracts of land. Their moral condition is not very good. As to religion, neither Moses nor his people profess any.

Joseph's Band of *Nez Perces* reside in the Nespelim valley, and with very few exceptions live in tents the year through. They are not industrious. Their moral and sanitary condition is not good. They profess no religion. Scrofula and constitutional syphilis is very prevalent yet I think there has been a decided improvement during the last year, as a number of them have brought logs to the mill, which have been sawed into lumber, with which they wish to build houses: and I firmly believe they would be in a better condition if the Government would stop issuing them rations.

The *Colville* and *Lake* tribes, residing in the north, are good people, well advanced in civilization. They are religious, belonging to the Catholic Church. Their moral condition is good. They have beautiful farms, well cultivated, live in good houses, all wear citizens' clothes, and I do not remember to have seen a long-haired Indian among the males. Their children are neatly dressed and many talk English. Yet they are not a healthy class of people. The seed of consumption and scrofula seems to be widely sown. While among the Colvilles I visited their church and the burying ground adjoining. There I counted ten new graves, mostly all little children. Both the Colvilles and the Lakes requested me to report their condition to the Department, and to intercede in their behalf that a physician be appointed to reside among them.

The Lower *Spokanes.*—Of these people I can only speak with praise. They are all Christians, belonging to the Presbyterian Church. Morally they are good. They are very industrious, living in good houses, on finely cultivated farms with their irrigating ditches. Yet, like the Lakes and Colvilles, their health is not good. The same diseases, consumption and scrofula, are widely spread. They also earnestly requested me to ask that a physician be appointed to reside among them.

Hospital.—In all this vast reservation there is no hospital of any kind. The various epidemics that visit the Indians and the poor facilities that an agency physician has to combat disease are very strong arguments in favor of a hospital being erected. One is needed very badly. Here is a large field for eye surgery, but for want of a suitable place to perform the operations in, little can be done, as it would be dangerous to attempt any delicate operation in an Indian house or tepee. Also, a great many cases that do not come under the notice of the physician until they have passed into the chronic stage or death has set its seal already upon the patient would be seen and treated in the first stages, as I feel sure that the Indians would in a short time avail themselves of the great benefits they would derive from a hospital.

As to the location of a hospital, right here in the Nespelim valley, within $1\frac{1}{2}$ miles of the mill, there is a most desirable location. There is a full half section of beautiful level land located at the base of the mountain, so situated that the sun shines upon it from the time it rises until it sets; and on the side of the mountain, five or six hundred feet above, there gushes forth the finest spring of clear, cold water that I have ever seen. I think it equals the great spring located at Huntsville, Ala. Here, with little expense, could be made a paradise. There are no mosquitoes, and during the day the wind comes up the valley from the Columbia, and at night it reverses and comes down the valley from the mountains. This spring will supply water sufficient for hospital, school, fountains, and much to spare. Also, the entire tract of land can be irrigated from the Little Nespelim : I earnestly call your attention to the importance of this matter.

The medicine man.—Speaking of this individual, I will briefly refer to my first acquaintance with these people. It was in January, 1890, that I first came among them. Within a very short time an epidemic of influenza and pneumonia broke out. They were all afraid to trust me. The medicine man was king of all he surveyed, telling the people it was a Boston (their term for white man) sickness, and I had brought it amongst them. The sweat house and cold bath were in full sway. The mortality became very great. Finally I

62 Quiotsa, c1903. Quiotsa was a relative of Chief Moses, possibly a brother. He is depicted here in his ceremonial clothes as a shaman or medicine man and carrying his sacred staff and medicine blanket

63 Doctor, buggy and dogs. This is taken from a glass negative in the Photography Collection at the University of Washington Library. L. D. Lindsley's notebook identifies the man as Dr O'Shea; there were a number of doctors in the O'Shea family of Spokane, but none of their ages as recorded in Spokane newspapers and the like seem to correspond with this person. An elderly present-day Indian resident of Nespelem identified the man orally as Dr Hodnutt, but no record of such a name could be found in Indian Service listings. Dr James Walker was a friend of Latham's. It is likely that in good weather Dr Latham traveled by buggy during his later years on the reservation

succeeded in getting control of a few cases that were given up to die and abandoned by the great medicine man, and with the assistance of Mr. Bouska, the miller, who could converse fluently with them, I was fortunate enough to save them, while their own doctor's cases were dying almost daily. Finally this individual became frightened. He informed them that the sickness was Boston sickness, and siwash medicine would not cure it. After that time I had my hands full, Mr. Bouska, acting as interpreter, going with me, and often seeing as many as 50 patients in one day. One of their medicine men and his family was taken sick. He sent for me, and fortunately they all recovered. Since that time I have had no trouble, and to-day their chief doctor, Timpasket, is one of my warmest friends. I have, during the past year, visited his family several times. To be sure they still practice a little in a certain way, but give me no trouble and never try to interfere with my cases. The sweat house is a great drawback, nearly every house having one, and the practice of indulging in these enervating sweats has been and is being discouraged as much as possible.

During the year I have treated 330 full-bloods, 8 half-breeds, and 2 whites, making in all 340 cases. I am happy to state there has been no epidemic of any kind, and the death list has been very low. Of the cases that I have been able to follow out but 7 have died, 4 children under 5 years of age; 1 from acute dysentery, 1 from hereditary syphilis, 1 from scrofula, and 1 from pneumonia; 3 cases over 5 years of age, 2 from consumption and 1 from progressive muscular atrophy. These deaths have all taken place here in the Nespelim valley amongst the Moses and Joseph Indians, except the case of progressive muscular atrophy, which occurred in the Spokane Reservation. The number of deaths that have taken place among the Colvilles, Lakes, and Lower Spokanes it is impossible for me to state, as I can not follow them to a termination.

Births.—Here in the Nespelim country, as far as I have been able to learn, there have been 9 children born, 4 males and 5 females. The Indian women are very superstitious in regard to this branch of the profession, and would die before they would submit to a white doctor attending them in confinement.

Medicines.—I do not like to enter complaints in this report, but I must say that the medicines sent are not in all cases what I would wish. The estimate I have made has not been followed out; some things that I wished very badly having been omitted; for instance, the hydrochlorate of cocaine, without which I am satisfied I never could have gained the confidence of these people. There are great sufferers from catarrhal conjunctivitis, which when neglected, in many cases has resulted in ptrygium, from which Chief Moses is a sufferer, and within in a year or two will lose the sight of one eye. Conjunctivitis, which is so widely spread amongst them, is due to smoke and alkali dust, and the proper use of cocaine gives wonderful relief. During the past year I have paid out $20 for this medicine alone. Some have called me a fool for doing it, but I feel well repaid, as I am sure I have saved two or three from blindness and given great relief to many. I sincerely hope this article will not be again overlooked when the next supply of medicines are shipped.

In conclusion, I desire to thank both you and Mr. A. M. Anderson, your clerk, for the assistance you have both rendered me in the prosecution of my duties; also the employés generally, for their uniform courtesy and affable manner.

I am, very respectfully,

E. H. LATHAM,
Agency Physician, Nespelim, Colville Reservation.

Whether in retaliation or response to his report, later in 1892 Latham was temporarily replaced at Nespelem and moved north to Tonasket on the Okanogan River. He was based there for over a year, treating patients, working in the new school, and getting to know Chief Tonasket's Okanogans, then still grieving for their aged leader who had died in April 1891. There, too, severe handicaps had to be endured: on March 11, 1893 Latham wrote to his Agent with a desperate plea for a matron to treat a batch of severe pneumonia cases and for his medical supplies to be rushed from the railhead at Wilbur. But, by this time, he was also keen to pursue interests quite apart from the Indians: "I have a sack of shot and my fishing rod at Goos Bills," he said, "please bring them." ("Wild Goose Bill" Condon was one of the earliest settlers in the region, and somewhat larger than life. In pre-reservation days he had traded guns to Chief Moses, had married two Indian women at different times, and was then busy promoting a property boom in the vicinity of the town of Wilbur, a landholding of his. He was a mixture of the elemental frontiersman and that other nineteenth-century type, the sporting man. In 1895 Wild Goose Bill was shot dead in a feud over a woman.)

Latham was quieter in his sporting pursuits, but it is obvious that he had a taste for the hunt, including the man hunt, and was able to indulge it a little in chasing the notorious Puckmiakin. Puckmiakin was an outlaw Okanogan who moved between the various camps on the reservation and the new, pretty lawless white communities around it; he bought and sold whisky and horses, horses to the whites in exchange for whisky, and whisky to the Indians in exchange for horses. He was shrewd, ruthless, and violent. In 1885 he axed open the head of Locos, one of Kamiakin's sons and a son-in-law to Chief Moses. For this and other crimes he was never resolutely punished by the law: such crimes fell within the jurisdiction of the State courts and the white authorities could not be bothered to spend white public money trying an Indian for offenses committed against other Indians. Again and again he was arrested for whisky trafficking and other crimes, only to be released to laugh in the faces of his captors. In 1890 he even escaped from a rowdy gang of white miners in the boom town of Ruby when his wife stripped to the waist and danced for the miners. In 1891, just off the reservation, near Ruby, Puckmiakin killed two of Chief Moses' band. Moses demanded his arrest and punishment, but once again he was arrested and then released. In August 1893 Puckmiakin's whisky was responsible for one of Chief Moses' nephews, Yayoskin or Jack O'Socken, killing his own brother by beating his brains out with a rock during a drunken row.

Latham wrote from Tonasket to the Acting Agent, Captain J. W. Bubb, on August 27:

> Immediately after the murder at Nespilem the Priest sent me word that likely Puck Mi a Kin would be at the church as there was to be a meeting the next day. Mr Strahl and I started at once thinking we might catch him he did not show up and from what we could learn from the Indians we concluded he had gone back to Nespilem, so we went there hoping to trail him down, for while we were at Nespilem he was on the Okanogan with whisky, and another murder was committed. The police caught the murderer who has been taken to the post by Mr Strahl. I am not acquainted with this Puck Mi A Kin but know him to be a very dangerous man, and think it will be hard to capture him. I think Smitkin and his people can get him if they will do so. they want him out of the way badly and I think can be induced to lay for him. Everything was quiet at Nespilem. Jack O Chaken says he knows he did wrong, but was drunk and did not know that he had killed his brother until the next day. he says he is willing to submit to any punishment, and I do not think it will be any trouble to capture him.

In fact, Yayoskin went unpunished and the following year, in another drunken frenzy, clubbed Chief Moses' sister, Shimtil, to death. He raced for the Canadian border, never to return. Puckmiakin, for his part, received his violent desserts rather more quickly: before the end of August 1893 he was struck down and killed by an Indian near a place at which he had so often traded, where the Okanogan River flows into the Columbia.

Alcohol was a scourge to the Indians. In a generation they had been uprooted, their own patterns of life were being destroyed and what remained was discouraged. They had to spend long tracts of time pent up, unable to roam and yet not equipped to farm adequately, or to do anything else. Whisky provided a pleasure of the moment, then oblivion. At the end of 1893, in submitting his request for medical supplies for the coming year, Latham wrote to his Agent as follows:

> You will notice that I have called for no Alchohol in this estimate and if the department will fill the estimate as I have made it out I can get along without it. The only place I dare use it amongst the Indians is in Liniments and they will then detect it sometimes and drink the entire bottle. With plenty of Oils, Castile Soap, ... Solution of Amonia, Chloroform, Camphor Gum, Glycerine and Turpentine I can make all the Liniment I need.

He then proceeded to report on an Indian who had had to be incarcerated in "the cooler" for a day. Clearly, by this time Latham had become acclimatized to the varied demands made upon him and thought that he largely understood the people he treated.

In June 1893 he wrote to agent Cole from Tonasket: "I would respectfully ask to be furnished with one copy of the Hon Commissioners Indian affairs report for 1892." This was the *Annual Report* which had printed Latham's report of medical conditions on the reservation. In that report he had asked for a hospital to be built at Nespelem; this had not materialized and, instead, he had been transferred to Tonasket. But in 1893 he may have believed that something more would be done at Nespelem. On August 3 Captain Bubb relayed a request to Washington, D.C., from Chiefs Moses and Joseph that Latham be returned to them at Nespelem, saying that they had "great faith in his treatment", and that they had severe need of a physician. He went back to Nespelem for Christmas 1893.

That winter proved to be another hard one: there was an outbreak of smallpox and many of the Indians refused to abide by Latham's vaccination scheme, especially Chief Joseph's band of Nez Perces, many of whom had died in Indian Territory when they had submitted to vaccination. Latham wrote to Captain Bubb to explain the failure of the scheme on March 1, 1894, adding, "Should you be in Spokane before you come here will you be so kind as to get . . . Five (5) pounds of the best tea." Ten days later he was reporting on a serious dispute which had erupted between Chief Moses' Columbias and Chief Joseph's Nez Perces. The two chiefs were old friends but the strain of feeling pent up in what must have seemed close proximity was beginning to tell. It was exacerbated by the pending opening of the North Half of the Colville Reservation to white prospectors and settlers: both chiefs could believe that land for Indians was becoming scarcer, that they would have to compete for it, and both could feel that they should be rewarded for accepting its loss. In reporting their quarrels to Captain Bubb, Latham wrote, "Both sides are holding secret meetings . . . Some of the Moses meetings have lasted the entire night. Moses has got it into his head that he is going to get a lot of money for the Reservation and says that when the money comes he will not give Joseph any. I think they are just talking over their imaginary grievances." Opposition to the opening of the North Half was in fact widespread: in July Latham reported to the Agent that he had found one hundred and thirty-six Indians, probably San Poils and Nespelems, "opposed to the treaty"; also, they refused to be counted and refused to take any rations from the government.

In reporting on such matters Latham was clearly taking on responsibilities quite apart from questions of health. In April 1894 he wrote to the Agent to inform him of his negotiations with an Okanogan carpenter for fees to be charged for work at Nespelem. In November he was discussing the problems of the Nespelem flour mill and considering the merits of various gunpowders. By the following September, 1895, the doctor had become a sort of intermediary between Captain Bubb, the Agent, and the Indians at Nespelem; in this role he wrote on the 18th to ask if he should set those Indians willing to do so on cutting wood for the proposed school building. Latham's position was, in fact, formalized a few days later, on September 28, when Captain Bubb wrote to the government farmer at Nespelem to tell him that the doctor was his "representative at that station". For a while thereafter Latham was responsible for the receipt of supplies of all kinds—farm

implements, building materials, and so on—as well as for issuing rations,
reporting criminal activities, and supervising housebuilding. For the U.S.
Census in 1900 he was allocated the arduous task of enumerating the whole of
the Spokane Reservation. Later, in the autumn of 1906 he doubled as a teacher
in the Nespelem day school—until he could not continue teaching because of
the demands of sick Indians needing his attention.

Indeed, it is difficult to imagine precisely when the doctor had time to
attend to health matters. Yet the report he submitted halfway through 1895,
to give but one example, recounted a year full of medical activity, and at the
end of 1895 he and Dr James Walker, who was then based at Tonasket,
submitted a proposal for a fourth physician to be assigned to the reservation.
They wanted the new doctor to be located on Fourth of July Creek in the far
northeast of the reservation, which was inaccessible in winter both to Latham
and Walker and to the physician based at the Agency headquarters in the
southeast. Like the request for a hospital at Nespelem, this proposal seems to
have been ignored by the authorities in Washington, D.C. Latham had to
travel vast distances by horse—and, later, by wagon—to treat the sick, and
often had to camp out at night away from home; yet at least once, in 1897, a
request for forage for the extra horse necessitated by these sick visits had to be
forwarded all the way to Washington, D.C., for approval. Perhaps it is not
surprising that over the years Latham may well have given increasing
amounts of his time to outdoor pursuits—hunting, fishing, and, of course,
photography—and less to his job.

There were epidemics which demanded all of a doctor's energies. During
the winter of 1900 Latham had to contend with a vicious outbreak of
smallpox, especially among the Nez Perces. On January 19 the weather was
still mild, there was no snow on the ground and wild flowers were in bloom.
Then, an Indian named George Washington found a blanket on the road in
the course of a journey from Yakima, and it was this blanket which—Latham
believed—carried the disease. In no time fifteen cases were reported, then a
hundred. Washington survived to help the doctor, but his wife was the first to
die. Vaccination and quarantine were ordered, blankets were burned, houses
were fumigated, and disinfectants were used in profusion. Nevertheless, thirty
or so people died. There was gossip outside the reservation among whites to
the effect that Latham had not visited the quarantine area for five or six days.
Such rumors persisted.

On March 1, 1908 Latham wrote to the then Agent, a punctilious former
army man, Captain John McAdam Webster:

Dear Sir: Until very recently I did not know that there was dissatisfaction
in your office in regard to my treatment of the Indians. I think Captain that I
have tried to treat these people right. I am sure that no Indian can truthfully
say that I have ever refused to go to see them when called uppon. It is true
that there have been Indians sick that I did not see and new nothing about
but they failed to notify...me...that they wanted or needed me now these
very ones are the ones that will put a pitiful story and say I neglected them.

I am sure there has never been an epidemic of any kind that I have not
been right out in the thickest of it from beginning to end. When we had the
Small Pox in 1900 here I held the quarantine, was with them day after day
and after it was over I thoroughly disinfected them so that there was no
relapse, and the next year 1901 the same disease broke out on the Spokane

Reservation I was called there and went from house to house and vaccinated them all and I stayed right up there in the snow and saw the thing through.

This has been the hardest winter I have ever experienced I have not been well but I have been out day after day and our epidemic of Gripp is over, with no deaths . . .

Earlier in Captain Webster's time as Agent there had been press rumors about the doctor's competence—and, certainly, as early as 1893 Latham had once been asked to explain and support a diagnosis to Washington, D.C. Also, Captain Webster had some knowledge of Latham's drinking problem; on January 23, 1905 the doctor had penned the following to him:

The weather here is very disagreeable the snow is about a foot deep and today it is raining hard. I am like you I do not like snow or Sleigh riding and it is strange how our tastes are alike in regard to Spring flowers and Mint juleps, but Captain I have reformed and am strictly on the Water Wagon. I am giving these fellows all good advise and offering myself as the terrible example.

On the other hand, Captain Webster knew that Latham was always ready to request aid for financially afflicted Indians. Indeed, just a few days after his declaration that he was on the "Water Wagon", Latham wrote on February 3 about certain "old and indigent" Indians at Nespelem, and the various Bureau of Indian Affairs files contain many such letters from him; between April and June of 1895 alone he had sent in four of these requests. Captain Webster weighed the various factors in the balance when he composed his staff efficiency report of 1909:

> Is a superannuated gentleman who has not kept up with his profession, and has vegetated and hibernated at Nespelem for the past 18 years; is kindly, hospitable and charitable; has accumulated enough money to buy a nice place on Lake Chelan, which has increased in value since he purchased it. He has exhibited more energy in the past year, but is too old and indolent to be efficient, and I rate him "Fair".

Whatever Latham's medical record, he claimed to have been befriended by a number of influential Indians, especially Chief Moses of the Columbias, Chica-ma-poo, the oldest survivor among Chief Joseph's band at Nespelem, and Chief Joseph himself. The doctor probably did maintain friendly relations with Chief Moses, who was unfailingly courteous and diplomatic and, despite his occasional recourse to one of his own "medicine men", had sufficient faith

65 Albert Waters' winter quarters, c1901. Note the mixture of reed mats and canvas in the construction of this composite tepee

in white medicine by 1894 to allow Latham to vaccinate his people against smallpox. Chief Moses let Latham treat his own eyes for catarrhal conjunctivitis by the application of hydrochlorate of cocaine to relieve the pain. When the aged Columbia died in March 1899, his passing was commemorated in a large-scale potlatch that June which was attended by many hundreds of Indians from throughout the Pacific Northwest. Moses' senior wife, Mary, gave away many of the Chief's possessions, including a fine coat and war bonnet to Chief Joseph and a pair of decorated horns to Latham, who photographed the proceedings. It may have been on that occasion that he made some of his portraits of Columbia women and of certain of Chief Moses' relatives.

Chica-ma-poo prided herself on her independence and lived alone at Nespelem during her last years. A report in the Spokane *Spokesman–Review* of April 16, 1905 recorded that though she was very ancient, her teeth were "sound and her step as light as a young woman's". Her tepee was very near to Latham's house and, as she suffered a number of fractures—including, apparently, both wrists—he must have seen her frequently. He prided himself on the fact that she never asked for payment for the privilege of taking her likeness, whereas other photographers, including Lee Moorhouse, were so charged. In her very old age, according to the *Spokesman–Review*, she took to visiting the Agency buildings each day and sat on the porch for the entire day, saying nothing; if she was eventually put out without being given food, she would call Latham "all the opprobrious Indian names" she could think of, "the worst in the language being 'bad'." "One day," the report continued, "the doctor missed the old woman . . . and, taking some rice and salmon, he went to her tepee. Here he found her . . . eating a biscuit and with a club beating off a half dozen mongrel dogs who were endeavoring to take it from her." Clearly, from the point of view of an age slightly less intolerant of the needs of old people, the relationship between the doctor and this very old and crippled woman is ambiguous; Latham liked to think that she submitted to his camera "with the vanity of her sex" because, as he told her, she would soon be dead and forgotten, "but if they had a picture of her they could look at it and say, 'This is poor old mama'."

Similar conflations of genuine charity, self-interest, medical duty and historical curiosity seem to have motivated Latham's relationship with Chief Joseph. On June 30, 1895 he reported to the Agent as follows:

> During the Winter Chief Joseph had a very severe case of Pneumonia and at first refused to be treated by me and I think would surely have died had it not been for Chief Peo who was visiting here. he talked with him and the Nez Perces until he sent for me and after that I waited on him constantly for several weeks it was a hard fight but he recovered and since then I have had no trouble with his tribe. If any are sick and do not let me know, he comes himself and goes with me to see that the medicine is taken according to directions.

After the Nez Perce Chief's death in 1904 Latham continued to stress his treatment of the Chief's pneumonia. The newspaper feature article titled "Choosing Chief Joseph's Successor", which appeared in *The Oregon Sunday Journal* for Christmas Day 1904, includes the following quotation from Latham:

66 Profile of Yellow Bull, June 1905. Yellow Bull wears a fine red robe trimmed with ermine. It is said that when he delivered his oration for the dead Chief Joseph he wore the dead man's eagle headdress and rode his favorite horse; as this photograph was taken during those commemorative events this eagle hat may, therefore, have once belonged to Joseph

Joseph was a true Indian. One instance of the manner in which he did business will illustrate this. For years I had befriended Joseph and nursed him as if he were a child when he had pneumonia, and had fed him from my cellar when he was in need of food. Knowing this I thought there would be little trouble in inducing Joseph to pose for a photograph. Joseph demurred. There is no use hurrying an Indian. Some days later I mentioned it again. He refused flatly. Winter came on. He got out of food. I gave him a sack of potatoes and mentioned the picture. He grunted. I gave him another sack of potatoes two weeks later and again I mentioned the picture. He said, "Sometime" . . . Then I gave him two sacks of potatoes and $5. He promised to dress in all his regalia and go to some wild spot on the river and pose for the picture. On the first pretty day, the time agreed upon for taking the picture, I appeared, camera in hand, but Joseph didn't even grunt. I

appealed to his squaws. One of them began jabbering and going for him in true squaw fashion. I heard her mention the potatoes several times over. Then he got up and said "All right", and the pictures here given was the result.

Similar condescension appeared in Latham's earlier newspaper comments on the Chief's death, "Chief Joseph's End Due To His Grief", and he was even more forthright when he wrote to Professor Meany on January 20, 1902. The Professor had asked him to photograph the Chief with his two wives. In his reply Latham stressed the low esteem in which women were held by the Nez Perces, concluding, "As grasping and selfish as old Joseph is, I do not think any inducement could be brought to bear to have his portrait taken with his women. Old Chief Moses was just the opposite," he continued, "he was always proud of Mary and on all occasions would tell what a good woman she was, he never went any place without her and she always drove the horses and took care of the money." It is not surprising, perhaps, that Latham felt—as he put it in "Chief Joseph's End Due To His Grief"—that "Joseph was an Indian in many ways. He always harbored jealousy, and I am convinced he never liked any white man."

67 White visitors, Indian camp, July 4, Nespelem, 1900s

68 *Opposite* Nespelem Falls. This is just one of a series of spectacular leaps taken by the Nespelem River in its descent to the Columbia

69 Spokane River

70 *Below* The Agency, Nespelem, c1910

Whether the Nez Perce leader harbored jealousy or not, it does seem to be the case that he did not like Latham. In November 1901 he went so far as to seek the doctor's dismissal, along with that of the then Agent, Albert M. Anderson, and the government farmer at Nespelem, Thomas McCrossen. He claimed that Anderson was prejudiced against him, that McCrossen had refused to issue rations, and that Latham did not visit the sick in their homes. Anderson was eventually dismissed from the Indian Service for irregularities in the accounts and McCrossen had, in fact, not issued rations in an effort to force the Chief to send the Nez Perce children to boarding school. It is therefore likely that there was some truth in the charge against Latham.

Nevertheless, when the famous Chief died, Latham was on hand to comment in the press and to photograph the various leaders who contended for the right to succeed him. These included William Andrews, Albert Waters and Peo-peo Tholekt. (It may be that Peo-peo Tholekt was the very Peo who had persuaded Chief Joseph to let Latham treat his pneumonia.) Albert Waters secured the appointment and Latham must have been gratified to know that he had earlier made a good picture of the new Chief's winter quarters, just as at the same time he had photographed Chief Joseph's own tepees. Latham was

72 Young married couple.
The feather tied in this
manner in the man's hair
indicates his married status

also present at the ceremonies attendant upon the reburial of Chief Joseph in
June 1905, when a monument was erected over the new grave. At that time he
captured a fine likeness of Yellow Bull who, though now blind, had come to
deliver his oration for his old companion in war and exile.

Latham made a point of taking pictures at most of the Indian Fourth of July
celebrations held at Nespelem during the early years of the twentieth century.
He also liked to get away from Nespelem—to his house on Lake Chelan for
about a month each summer, and to the surrounding mountains and rivers.
While out hunting and fishing he made many views, especially of Nespelem
Falls, Okanogan landscapes and the Columbia and Spokane Rivers. But he
always returned to Indians and Agency scenes, such as the horse brands burnt
into the blacksmith's door, the sawmill, his own office, and, above all, people
in their finery.

It is most likely that Latham spent ever-increasing parts of his days on
photography, so that on retirement in 1910 he must have had plenty to do
with his hobby. Except for a possible brief period back on the Colville
Reservation as a stand-in doctor in 1911, his last years were spent in the quiet
of his house on Lake Chelan. He died in March 1928.

4 The Photographs

"The finest collection ... in the Northwest"

Precisely when Latham began to take photographs is not known, but it must have been before 1890 because the earliest known picture by him (plate 73) is so dated in his own inimitable handwriting and spelling. It depicts a rather hapless-looking man exhibiting some grand produce at a fair in Spokane, commercial center of the country encircled by the "Big Bend" of the mighty Columbia River; the caption reads "Watermills Grain & Vegetables Part of Exhibit at Spokane Falls 1890". In all likelihood, Latham taught himself the art while resident in Cincinnati before migrating westwards. As a trained pharmacist and doctor, he had ready access to the necessary chemicals and would have easily acquired expertise in using them. In fact, the advanced world over, there were disproportionate numbers of doctors and allied workers among late nineteenth-century amateur photographers, especially among those located off the beaten track. Two such contemporaries of Latham were Dr P. H. Emerson in rural East Anglia, England, and Dr Charles Louis Gabriel of Gundagai, a wayside Australian country town. All of Latham's photographic life fell within the era of the gelatin dry plate, which began in about 1880 and continued until 1920 and beyond. It is not known what camera he used, but it must have been a relatively small and handy one because those of his negatives which survive are all 4 × 5in glass plates. (There are some 5 × 7in glass plates of his images, but these may be copy negatives.)

Latham was essentially an *amateur* photographer. His name figures in no list of commercial photographers issued in his own time and, probably because of the remoteness of Nespelem (it did not officially become a town until the establishment of a post office there in 1899), he appears not even to have joined any of the camera clubs which were becoming established at the turn of the century. His amateur status did not, however, prevent him selling, or attempting to sell, copies of his pictures. In June 1901 Latham met Professor Edmond S. Meany, the historian and himself a keen amateur photographer. Meany was writing a thesis on Chief Joseph and also planning a biography. While on a brief visit to Nespelem to meet the Chief, Professor Meany became friendly with Latham, who gave him some of his Indian pictures. The two men corresponded thereafter, and in November 1902 Latham offered Meany's friends Indian pictures for "$4.00 per dozen unmounted or $5.00 mounted".

How many prints Latham dispatched to Professor Meany is unknown, but those that survive are all of the common velox type, mostly 4 × 5in, usually semi-matt in finish, and often mounted on gray card. When the historian died he left an enormous number of photographs to the University of Washington; the Photography Collection in the Suzzallo Library there contains hundreds of images from the Meany Bequest, and many of them

73 Watermelons, grain and vegetables, Spokane, 1890. This is Latham's earliest known photograph and was made during the Northwestern Industrial Exposition, the first major exhibition of the region's life and resources

include annotations in the historian's own hand which are almost always a reliable guide to the subject matter and/or origin of the picture. On one or two of the images by Latham, Meany recorded their maker's name and, where he did not, their origin at the doctor's hands could sometimes be established by relating them to letters by Latham in the files of Professor Meany's correspondence, which is also preserved in the University of Washington Libraries.

Latham gave away many pictures. In July 1903 he sent his Agent, Albert M. Anderson, a batch of photographs "to fill out" his collection; sometimes he appears to have donated or sold whole albums of his work. The library of a private club in Seattle has an album containing a dozen of his prints with a printed title to the effect that it had been made by "Dr. Edward H. Latham of Nespelem Washington". This album includes the portrait of "Chief Joseph in war costume" (plate 4) which Latham copyrighted in 1903. Some twenty of the doctor's images also appear in the first of a number of albums compiled by Thomas Prosch, a prominent turn of the century Seattle newspaperman and amateur historian; the handwritten captions under some of these pictures, mostly taken in about 1903, also credit them to Latham. The Prosch albums are preserved in the University of Washington Photography Collection.

The images that survive must be but a small proportion of those made by the physician. In one letter to Professor Meany, Latham said, "I have some four or five dozen plates exposed which I will try to develop before I go . . . into the mountains." Multiply this by, perhaps, twenty years of photographic activity and it is obvious that Latham must have made many hundreds, possibly thousands, of pictures. In 1977 the Photography Collection at the University of Washington was fortunate enough to acquire a large file of negatives and pictures from the family of a very important Northwest professional photographer, Lawrence D. Lindsley. This collection included many prints of Latham images and, more importantly, several hundred of the doctor's glass negatives; moreover, these were accompanied by a notebook in Lindsley's hand which credits the negatives to Latham and identifies the subject matter of the pictures by number. Often the annotations are historically unreliable, making it clear that the entries were composed by Lindsley for his own benefit, rather than by Latham to jog his own memory. (Such wholesale acquisition of the work of one photographer by another is not uncommon in the history of photography.) At any rate, Lindsley, as the negatives attest, copyrighted some of the pictures under his own name (and may have published these), cropped a few, and achieved special effects with others.

Very many of the pictures in Lindsley's file of Latham's negatives are most interesting, but probably not worth reproducing in a book like this. These include views of a Presidential Peace Medal presented to Chief Joseph, of a white girl in Indian dress and, more important from the aesthetic point of view, numerous variants of several of the portraits; for instance, there are almost a dozen pictures of Elijah Williams, Chief David Williams' son, all taken at the same time and all slightly different. More tantalizing is the fact that some of the negatives for which there are written annotations appear to be missing: negative number 4803 is "Group of people at Nespelem ready to hunt"; such a group might well have included Latham himself.

It is possible that Lindsley acquired the negatives from Latham himself. According to Mary Latham's obituary in the January 21, 1917 edition of the Spokane *Spokesman–Review* he spent his last years at Lakeside, Chelan

County, and during some of those years, if the appropriate directory is to be believed, Lindsley, then a budding photographer, was also a Lakeside resident. However, there must have been many negatives that Lindsley did not acquire. Mr Bob Eddy of Cashmere, Washington, a former resident of Nespelem and an enthusiast for Native American history, recalled in July 1977 that Mrs Grace Christiansen Gardner Wenzel (who, as a girl, had known Chief Moses) found two apple-boxes of glass negatives in the basement of a derelict Nespelem store in about 1938. She took a few and intended to return for the rest, but meantime the store burned down. She gave Mr Eddy copies of the prints she made and, from these, it is clear that they overlap, but do not duplicate, the Lindsley negatives. The present location of the negatives discovered by the late Mrs Wenzel is unknown, but prints of the pictures may be seen at the local museums in Cashmere and Moses Lake, Washington.

So far, only one other significant collection of images attributable to Latham has been found: in the Library of Eastern Washington State Historical Society in Spokane is a large batch of recently made prints, sometimes credited to Edward S. Curtis, which in style and subject matter seem to overlap with pictures in the Lindsley collection; they could conceivably have been made from negatives missing from the Lindsley file. But several other

74 Nespelem Falls

prints of Latham images do appear, and in various collections. In Spokane Public Library, for example, in the general Indians file and elsewhere, there are a number of pictures which appear to be by Latham, including one of Professor Meany delivering an oration at the reburial of Chief Joseph in June 1905. And in Eastern Washington State Historical Society there is the print reproduced in this book of some Indian girls playing with a captive bear (plate 30). Also, several of the pictures credited to T. W. Tolman in the Montana Historical Society collections at Helena, Montana, are in fact by Latham. One of these shows the monument to Chief Joseph erected at his reburial and taken, by the look of it, just after the monument had been put up, on the occasion when Professor Meany—and, of course, Chief Yellow Bull—delivered their commemorative speeches.

Nothing seems to be known about the Tolman to whom these pictures were credited, but there is a Mount Tolman to the east of Nespelem on the Colville Reservation. As other landmarks there were named after early white settlers—Goose Flats in the southwest corner for Wild Goose Bill Condon, for instance, or Strahl Canyon just south of the Columbia for Arthur Strahl, a one-time government farmer—it is possible that Tolman was an early resident in the region and, therefore, a neighbor to the doctor. A note on the back of one of the prints made from Latham's better-known portrait of Chief Joseph in the Indians file at the University of Washington Photography Collection reads: "Picture taken by Thomas W. Tolman for Dr. Ed. Latham (Indian agent at Nespelem) who had picture copyrighted." It is likely that there is a simple confusion here: both the copyright-file print of this particular picture and the former copyright-file picture of Quiotsa, Chief Moses' relative, which are now in the National Anthropological Archives, Washington, D.C., have notes on their backs to the effect that they were copyrighted by Tolman in 1903. As it is certain that Latham made these pictures, it seems likely that he took them *for* Tolman, or partly for Tolman, who had them copyrighted. Somehow, the reverse story got abroad and, it seems, was generally believed. (The copyrighting of other people's work is also quite common in the history of photography, and was certainly not necessarily an unfriendly gesture.)

The reason for recounting some of these problems of authorship and authenticity in such detail is to establish definitively that this previously virtually unknown photographer was the creator of the images reproduced in this book. If this is so, they are the product of a single vision which can be described. On the other hand, the very existence of these problems signifies that Latham was an amateur photographer without an *obvious* photographic style, and this is a fundamental matter which will be of some concern in the descriptive analysis which follows.

The landscapes are in some ways the least significant of Latham's photographs and, in comparison with other areas of his endeavor, such as portraits, few survive. Nevertheless, they do reveal certain characteristics which recur elsewhere. What is immediately noticeable about the landscapes is that they are extremely limited in range—just rivers and waterfalls. Also—and this cannot be demonstrated in this book—the negative files contain very many images of almost precisely the same view; Nespelem Falls as viewed in plate 74, for instance, was chosen almost arbitrarily for reproduction here from a batch of negatives markedly similar to one another. It could be that this simply indicates that Latham was lacking in confidence, that he was not sure that he had caught the scene the first time, or even the second and third time. Yet he was, it seems, more than proficient technically; light on a rush of water does present problems, especially if the waterfall or stream is in a half-darkened glen, such as is depicted in plates 61 and 74, but Latham always appears to have solved such problems. Consequently, what must have fascinated him, made him return again and again, was the very fluidity of water itself, its effervescence, its ever-changing yet continuous nature, as if the land through which it flows were static and moribund.

Latham returned repeatedly to Nespelem Falls, a place where the Nespelem River takes a series of extraordinary leaps in its descent towards the not-too-distant Columbia, especially during the spring run-off when the melted snows of winter make for the sea. The general topography of the Colville Reservation is one of irregular hills—mountains in places—and scattered pines. Around Nespelem, and in many other sections, there is no definite place for the eye to rest, as it were—except on water. In the winter this landscape is, literally, blanked out by snow. And in summer it is beaten like an anvil by a harsh sun; for the most part, undifferentiated brightness fills every space, defeats the sense of perspective in everything but the massive and, of course, the moving.

The general undifferentiated brightness is sometimes broken by threatening storm clouds, especially in late summer. Latham, starved of that subtlety of light which so delights photographers, was clearly interested in such episodes; in a picture like "Indian Camp, July 4 celebrations" (plate 75), the controlling feature is the sense of drama provided by the shadows over the land. It may have been a vision of the landscape like that described above which motivated Latham to leave man out of his pictures of it. In reality, this land was largely empty of people, and he chose to present it in that way; his camera caught the thing itself, the flow of the stream, the cascade of water and light. When there is a figure in the landscape it is not there to suggest a philosophical statement about man's relationship to his environment but to record scale; for example, plate 76 shows a man standing on a rocky outcrop beside the falls, his tiny figure emphasizing the height of the cascade.

Latham's landscapes of towns or encampments are similarly devoid of people. They seem even more so because of his treatment of the foreground. With each photograph he clearly had a notion of how much he wanted to get within the verticals of the frame: to the edge of the circle of tepees in plate 1, for example, or all the town buildings in his view of Nespelem township (plate 59). This alone determined the distance of his camera from the subject and, therefore, the amount of space in the foreground. The average professional photographer—or, indeed, many an amateur photographer—would have provided a line into the picture, something to traverse that empty space: a fallen tree, say, or a ridge of land, a wagon to the right or left. Except in such shots as that of the Agency (plate 70), where he seems to have attempted something along these lines in that the avenue of fruit trees marginally reduces the distance the eye must travel before reaching the jauntily posed man, Latham rarely chose to curtail the distancing effect of these foreground spaces. In several of his pictures such deliberate distancing is marvelously effective: Nespelem township was then but a few flimsy wooden buildings in the vastness of the land, and that is how it *must* be seen in Latham's photograph of it. Again, the empty foreground in some of the views of Indian encampments serves to thrust them down into the valley, thus making them

75 Indian Camp, July 4 celebrations, Nespelem, 1900s. Inside the circle of tepees the parade is being conducted; at that time at least two hundred riders participated

appear to nestle in the palm, so to speak, of the hills. On the other hand, the emptiness of these spaces is sometimes uncanny, seemingly uncalled for; basically, it tends to alienate the viewer from what is going on in the middleground of the picture. In a sense, some of these views strain for the effect of an aerial photograph; this is especially true of the view of Fort Spokane (plate 21). In some of the shots of the July 4 celebrations (for example, plate 75) it is easy to see that something is happening: horse-riders are circling within the ring of tepees, people are participating in the events; the viewer, however, is prevented from participating. In reality, on such occasions whites could not fully participate, however much their presence was tolerated, because in so many respects these festivals were reaffirmations of Indian cultural identity. Therefore, it may be that in achieving an alienating effect in these views, Latham was more precise than he knew.

Some of the photographs of these celebratory events taken from closer in convey a similar alienating effect, but it is caused by other means. The line of chiefs, one with a gun (plate 77), was clearly created to play on the viewer's expectations about the fierceness, the warrior heritage, of feathered braves. In some ways, such a picture is reminiscent of the re-creation photographs of Edward S. Curtis, e.g., "Apsaroke War Group", or "The Spirit of the Past" (plate 78). But there is a major difference: in Curtis' shots the Indians are totally involved in the process of re-creation, and the viewer observes their drama almost with them, with a sense of participation; the Indians in Latham's recreation views not only look to the camera, but seem wooden, transfixed, as if waiting for instructions from the photographer. The viewer, in other words, is excluded, because all the interaction, the actual drama, is with the photographer. Something of the same sort happens, if to a lesser extent, in

77 Chiefs. The figure in the center is Joe Moses and the one on the far right is Cool-Cool-a-Weela; between them is an Indian policeman

76 *Opposite* Nespelem Falls. Note the man and dog on the outcrop of rock halfway up the picture, giving a clue to the height of the falls

78 "The Spirit of the Past",
by Edward S. Curtis. This
Apsaroke or Crow group was
taken in 1905

certain of the portraits. The very title of "Chief Joseph in war costume" indicates a slight straining for drama, in that it was taken in peacetime, and the horseback shot of the Chief catches him at a moment of discomfort, so to speak, as if he is not at ease in his regalia.

The above is intended as a description, not as an overbearing value judgement; indeed, as will be apparent, interaction between subject and photographer proves to be one of the most outstanding qualities of many of Latham's other portraits. The truth of the analysis is borne out when the views of July 4 celebrations without an alienating effect are examined. It seems to be the case that these are all action shots: horsemen galloping by, a group of women parading in full traditional dress, or drummers inside the circle of spectators. The photographer set up his camera just off the horsetrack (plates 79 and 80), say, or just inside the circle of spectators (plate 81), and the action continued. In other words, precisely because a continuous activity was unfolding, the very presence of the photographer was effaced. This contrast could be formulated as follows: the viewer's sense of alienation increases, if not in an easily quantifiable manner, according to the degree of control exercised or attempted by the photographer.

This is an appropriate juncture to look in some detail at the largest group of Latham's work, the portraits. At first glance it might be thought that these are just so many Indian pictures, indistinguishable from others: a woman with a bead bag here, a man in an eagle hat there; the postures of a bygone era, untitled records of a largely anonymous people, akin to snapshots, picture postcards. And it is certainly the case that Latham's pictures can be looked through in vain for portraits with the kind of romantic aura that is associated with those of Curtis or, to a lesser extent, Adam Clark Vroman. Moreover, his photographs lack the variety of pose and activity that can be found in the work of such lesser artists as Lee Moorhouse, John Anderson, or L. A. Huffman. Thus it is that it could be assumed that Latham was a photographer without an obvious photographic style. In fact, the reverse is true.

The most notable aspect of the portraits is that they are all full-figure. There are no close-ups of faces or, even, views to waist-level. Except in the cases of Yellow Bull (plate 66) and Charlie Wilpocken (plate 50), there is not even the luxury of a profile. In each photograph the frame encompasses the whole figure (and, sometimes, a horse or a tepee, too) together with what appears at first to be an almost random amount of space around the figure. The camera was held at eye-level, so that there is minimal manipulation in this respect; the subjects are not aged by being looked down upon or heightened, made prouder, by being looked up at. Similarly, they are set pretty squarely within the frame, moving, as it were, neither up out of it nor downwards. All this suggests that Latham was not primarily concerned with what has often seemed to be the essential business of the portrait maker, the capture of the subject's "character", or the recording of a particularly interesting or haunting expression of the moment. This does not mean, of course, that Latham never caught these things (note the degree of intensity and awe in the face of the young man in plate 82, for example), but that his typical achievement resides elsewhere. In his portraits the viewer's eye may move to the eyes of the subject, but often it will roam over the picture as a whole as if it were all on the same plane and all its parts granted the same degree of importance. It becomes a kind of still life. Thus, the objects which attend a person—a woman's moccasins, a man's beaded vest, a blanket, a cornhusk

79 Parade, Men's Division,
July 4, Nespelem, 1900s

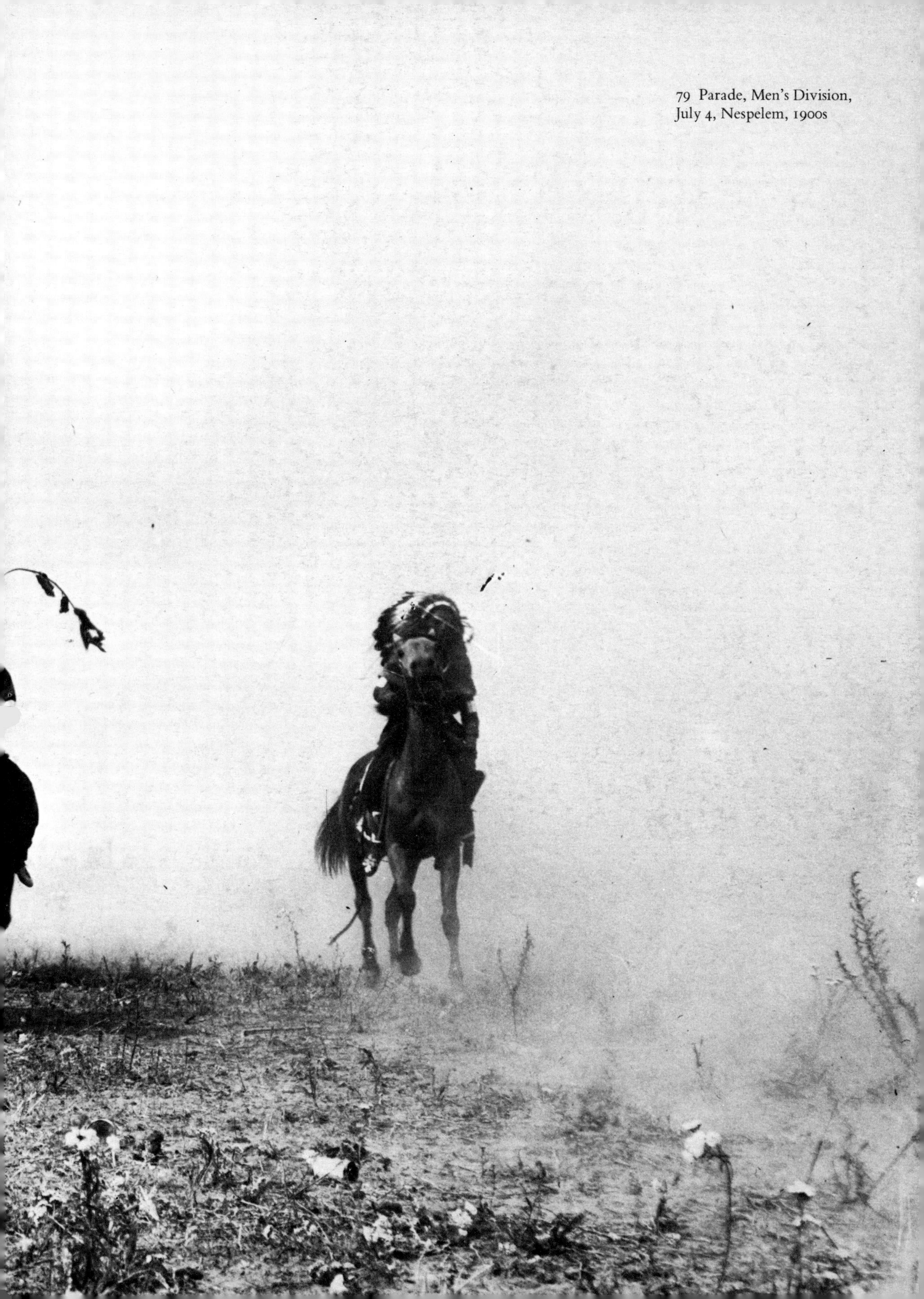

80 Parade, Women's
Division, July 4, Nespelem,
1900s

81 Drummers, July 4,
Nespelem, 1900s

82 Young man, *c*1903. This
young man also appears in
plate 72. The picture may
have been published and
credited to L. D. Lindsley

83 *Opposite* The bachelor's
friends. The "bachelor"
himself has not been
identified. He is almost
certainly the same person as
the man depicted in plate 63
and, therefore, probably
another U.S. Indian Service
physician, possibly Dr James
R. Walker, Latham's
contemporary

bag—assume a stress of their own. Indeed, it is conceivable that Latham was as much interested in these trappings as in the faces of his subjects. In "The bachelor's friends" (plate 83) the man is almost lost among his "friends", his dogs, guns and fishing gear. In several of the views of women with handiwork the woman seems positively to *present* her beaded bag as if this object, rather than her, were the true subject of the photograph. Perhaps the most striking examples of all are the babies in cradleboards (plates 5 and 84) propped against benches like inanimate matter, the human equivalents of the bachelor's gun or fishing rod; at the very least, it is arguable in each case whether the baby or the cradleboard is the picture's subject.

When there is a natural background in these pictures the photographer, for the most part, shows no interest in it; there is, perhaps, just sky for good light and an unrecognizable hillside. The maximum extent of his interest in natural backgrounds is indicated in a letter to Edmond Meany written on January 20, 1902 when he said, "If you could come here in the Spring I will try to get you any pictures you might wish. I would want to wait until after the leaves came out so as to get a good back ground and besides the light would be much stronger."

The lack of an interesting background, or one of just leaves, stops the eye at the person and his possessions. Indeed, it seems that whenever he could do so Latham provided a background which would do precisely that—the wall of his house, for example, or a hanging blanket. It is interesting to note that in the family portrait of the Wilpockens (plate 50) Charlie Wilpocken has been made to squat so that the rather low-hung blanket is still behind him.

At the turn of the century there was a convention that Indians should be photographed against natural textures—wool, beaten cedar-bark, or whatever. Both Curtis and Moorhouse did so. Latham worked within the convention and took it a stage further: many of his figures also stand on blankets or furs. This gives them a regal air; they have dominion over the natural world while at the same time they are subtly connected to that natural and, of course, Indian world—the animals they might hunt, fibres they might have woven or traded for. In other words, it would seem that the photographs render in visual terms a notion of Indians being intimately part of the organic world: the photographic and ethnographic import of the pictures is the same. This is particularly so in the "Mother and child" (plate 85) where the baby's cradleboard is strung up in the tree. The ethnographic information conveyed here is that babies are helped to keep cool by being raised into the breezes that wafted leaves encourage; the photographic information received is that, despite the grimace on the baby's face, mother, child and natural environment are all in harmony.

This mother and child probably do coexist in a slightly bizarre harmony, but generally the use of blankets behind a subject and furs or blankets underfoot creates a *dis*continuity between the subject and the natural world. While it is true that certain Indians sometimes spread skins on the ground to mark a place of transaction, it is still, after all, a very white idea to place a blanket on the ground to stand on, to make a special place for the photograph, to create a studio in nature. This, coupled with the previously observed flatness of these portraits, may mean that their subjects were considered as museum pieces.

It is noticeable that there is a preponderance of women and children in these pictures. Latham told Edmond Meany that when he first arrived at Nespelem

85 *Opposite* Mother and
child. The woman is Annie
from Wenatchee (plate 48)
and her child is also featured
in plate 84

86 Sisters

89 *Opposite* Young woman, blankets, and bead bag. The woman is probably Peo-na-nikt, a Nez Perce. The blankets are from Pendleton, Oregon, and made to patterns loosely based on Southwest Indian designs

90 Young boy, dressed up.

91 "Spirit Land". This is, of course, a double exposure of the women's division during a July 4 parade. It was probably accidental and may have been given its title by L. D. Lindsley rather than by Edward Latham. Nevertheless, it captures precisely the haunting quality to be found in so many of Dr Latham's photographs

he made a point of deliberately "making up" to the women and children in order to gain their confidence in him as a doctor and an entrée for himself into their homes. It might be thought that the portraits of women and children were, in consequence, a sort of by-product of this desire. However, it is just as likely that, as a photographer, Latham found the women and children more amenable than the men; certainly his irritation with a man who made his own terms with him is apparent in one of his letters to Meany about Chief Joseph:

> I got two negatives of Joseph, these I developed and they are good, but the old rascal fixed himself in a horrible shape, no one would know that it was Joseph, he painted himself ... dead black, was covered all with Eagle feathers, was riding a poor old bony horse he had ... the old scoundrel made me pay him ten dollars in advance, had I known how he was going to fix himself I would not have given him anything.

In sum, Latham's photographic vision is that of someone quite deeply alienated by the world around him, whether by the undifferentiated landscape where only water truly seems to live, or by the strange ceremonies of his Indian neighbors or by those people themselves. And yet he was constrained to photograph, again and again, the same subjects and in more or less the same way. In this he was not so much an amateur photographer as a folk or *primitive* artist, a kind of Edward Hicks of the camera who rendered not a series of peaceable kingdoms but a set of alien ones.

But this is too harsh. First, whether primitive or not, there is a directness, a face-to-face quality, a head-on quality about Latham's work which is very much part of the so-called "straight tradition" in American photography. It is this aspect of his work which relates his portraits both to E. J. Bellocq's "storyville portraits" of prostitutes in New Orleans and to those of the poor who stare so unflinchingly into the camera in Walker Evans' work of the 1930s. Thus, a picture like "Indian horsebrands" (plate 88), whatever it might tell us about ownership of Indian horses (and that is very little), has a *photographic* validity: it is an uncompromising study of line, texture, theme and variation, patterning.

Second, there is another virtue in this quality of directness. Whatever Latham's conscious or unconscious intentions, and despite the still-life tendency of his portraits, the humanity of the subjects cannot ultimately be evaded. We are aware that the baby in the cradleboard is not an object, that the young man cannot disguise his essentially human vulnerability before the mechanical eye of the camera, and that this woman, and that one, have a sense of pride in the things they have fashioned with their hands. In all probability Latham was not unusually compassionate, and it is virtually certain that he was, as Agent Webster said, only a "fair" doctor. But, as a photographer, Latham exercised the capacity—perhaps without ever knowing it—to render the essential humanity of the Indians who sat for him. He thus extends a little our awareness of history and the forms of man.

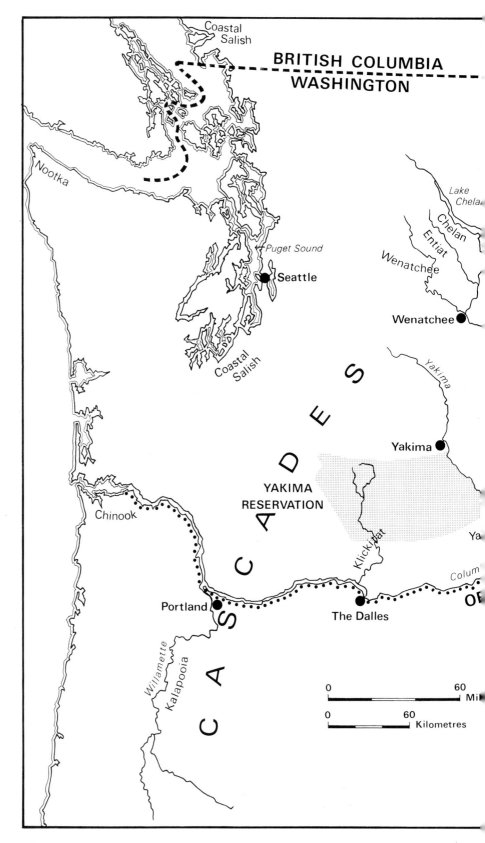

Coastal
Salish

BRITISH COLUMBIA
WASHINGTON

Nootka

*Lake
Chelan*

Chelan

Entiat

Wenatchee

Puget Sound

Seattle

Wenatchee

Coastal
Salish

C A S C A D E S

Yakima

Yakima

YAKIMA
RESERVATION

Chinook

Klickitat

Ya

Colum

Portland

The Dalles

OI

Willamette

Kalapooia

C A S C A D E S

0		60
		Mi

0		60
		Kilometres

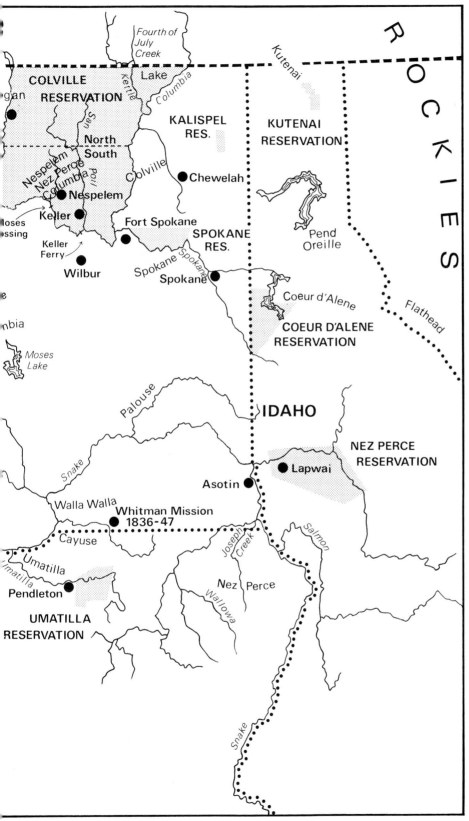

Sources

Not all the items consulted in the preparation of this book are recorded here; rather, the following includes materials actually reproduced or quoted, or relied upon either extensively or for significant details.

Photographs

The majority of photographs reproduced in this book were taken from glass negatives in the Lindsley Collection or from prints in the Indians file of the Photography Collection, Special Collections, Suzzallo Library, University of Washington, Seattle.

Exceptions are the following: plate 30 is reproduced from a print in the Eastern Washington State Historical Society Library, Spokane. Plates 45, 60, 77, and 93 are reproduced from prints in an album owned by the Rainier Club, Seattle. Plates 3 and 57 are reproduced from glass negatives in the Avery Collection, Manuscripts, Archives and Special Collections Division, Library, Washington State University, Pullman. Plate 78 is reproduced from a photogravure in Edward S. Curtis' *The North American Indian* (1907–30) owned by the Library of the University of Exeter, England.

Manuscripts

Letters by Edward H. Latham to Edmond S. Meany and the translation by Henry M. Steele are reproduced from the Edmond S. Meany Papers, University Archives and Records Center, University of Washington. Letters by Latham to agent John McAdam Webster are taken from the Webster Papers, Manuscripts, Archives and Special Collections Division, Washington State University Library. Other papers by or about Latham are from the Records of the Colville Reservation, Federal Archives and Records Center, Seattle.

Newspaper and Periodical Items

"Aged Amazon of the Nez Perces", *Spokesman-Review* (Spokane), April 16, 1905. Clipping in Eastern Washington State Historical Society Library.

Chase, Eugene B. "A Grand Aboriginal Function", *The Northwest Magazine*, XVII, No 8 (August 1899), pp 20–1.

"Chief Joseph's End Due to his Grief", *Spokesman-Review* (?), September 27, 1904. Clipping in Clarence Bagley Scrapbook, No 6, p 65, Northwest Collection, University of Washington Libraries.

"Dr. Latham Arrives at Inchelium", *Spokesman-Review*, February 22, 1911.

"Dr. Mary A. Latham", annual illustrated supplement to the Spokane *Spokesman*, 1892.

Joseph, Chief. "An Indian's View of Indian Affairs", *North American Review*, CXXVIII (April 1879), pp 412–33.

Moorhouse, Lee. "The Umatilla Indian Reservation", *The Coast*, XV, No 4 (April 1908), pp 235–50. (Includes photographs by Lee Moorhouse.)

Obituary for Edward H. Latham, *Spokesman-Review*, March 25, 1928.

Obituary for Mary A. Latham, *Spokane Chronicle*, January 20, 1917.

——. *Spokesman-Review*, January 21, 1917.

93 Joe Moses' headdress, c1903

154

"Smallpox Mostly a Scare", *Spokesman-Review*, March 19—. Clipping in Webster Papers, Washington State University Library.

Teit, James H. "The Middle Columbia Salish", *University of Washington Publications in Anthropology*, II (June 1928), pp 83–128.

Winner, Vella. "Choosing Chief Joseph's Successor", *Oregon Sunday Journal* (Portland), December 25, 1904. Clipping in McWhorter Collection, Washington State University Library.

Books

Annual Report of the Commissioner of Indian Affairs (Washington, 1889 and 1892.)

Brandon, William. *The American Heritage Book of Indians* (New York, 1961.)

Brown, Dee. *Bury My Heart at Wounded Knee: An Indian History of the American West* (New York, 1970; London, 1971.)

Brown, M. H. and W. R. Felton. *The Frontier Years* (New York, 1954; includes photographs by L. A. Huffman.)

Gidley, M. *The Vanishing Race: Selections from Edward S. Curtis' "The North American Indian"* (Newton Abbot and London, 1976; New York, 1977; includes photographs by Edward S. Curtis.)

Hamilton, Henry W. and Jean T. *The Sioux of the Rosebud: A History in Pictures* (Norman, Oklahoma, 1971; includes photographs by John A. Anderson.)

Hawthorne, Julian. *History of Washington: The Evergreen State from Early Dawn to Daylight*, Vol II (New York, 1893.)

Howard, Helen Addison and Dan L. McGrath. *War Chief Joseph* (1941) (Lincoln, Nebraska, 1964.)

Josephy, Alvin M. *The Nez Perce Indians and the Opening of the Northwest* (Abridged ed, New Haven and London, 1971.)

McLuhan, T. C. *Touch The Earth: A Self-Portrait of Indian Existence* (New York, 1971; London, 1973.)

McWhorter, Lucullus Virgil. *Yellow Wolf: His Own Story* (1940) (London, 1977.)

Newhall, Beaumont. *The History of Photography* (New York, 1964.)

Prucha, Francis Paul. *Americanizing the American Indians: Writings by the "Friends of the Indian" 1880–1900* (Cambridge, Massachusetts, 1973.)

Ruby, Robert H. and John A. Brown. *Half-Sun on the Columbia: A Biography of Chief Moses* (Norman, Oklahoma, 1965.)

Sandoz, Mari. *Cheyenne Autumn* (New York, 1953.)

Spier, Leslie. *The Prophet Dance of the Northwest and its Derivatives: The Source of the Ghost Dance.* General Series in Anthropology Number I (Menasha, Wisconsin, 1935.)

——. *The Sinkaietk or Southern Okanogan of Washington.* General Series in Anthropology Number VI (Menasha, Wisconsin, 1938.)

Spokane Falls Illustrated: A History of the Early Settlement (Minneapolis, 1889.)

Webb, W. and R. A. Weinstein. *Dwellers at the Source* (New York, 1973; includes photographs by Adam Clark Vroman.)

Weinstein, Robert A. and Larry Booth. *Collection, Use, and Care of Historical Photographs* (Nashville, 1977.)

Index

References to page numbers of picture captions appear in italics.